THE GENTILE ROOTS OF THE *Jewish Faith*

DAVID RAVENHILL

Offspring PUBLISHERS

www.offspringpublishers.com

Acknowledgements

I have never wavered from the belief that I'm a weak vessel, and that daily I depend upon the Lord for His strength. Not only have I come to rely upon the Lord but also His body the Church.

First of all I would like to thank my good friend and fellow soldier in Christ Ron Burtraw for his willingness to read through an early copy of this manuscript. Ron took the time to not only read but to make some important suggestions on how to improve the overall readability of this book.

Cheryl Ellicott has played a vital role in seeing this project come to birth. Cheryl not only edited and proofread the manuscript but also assisted me in the design of the cover. Without her expertise this book would still be sitting unfinished on my computer. Thank you Cheryl.

Table of Contents

Introduction

The title *The Gentile Roots of the Jewish Faith* is not intended to be provocative, but informative. Few believers understand the two thousand years of history before Israel's formation as a nation. If you mention topics such as the Tabernacle, sacrifices, priesthood, Sabbath, laws, altars, clean and unclean animals, most people immediately assume you're speaking about God's people Israel. But all of these topics are found within the first few chapters of Genesis — before the birth of Israel.

Here is how Arthur W. Pink refers to the first eleven chapters of Genesis. ' The first eleven chapters of Genesis are really *the foundation* on which rests the remainder of the Old Testament. They trace in rapid review the line of descent from Adam to Abram. It has been well said concerning the book of Genesis that "as the root to the stem so are chapters 1-11 to 12-50, and as the stem to the tree so is

Genesis to the rest of the Bible." One of the main purposes of Genesis is to reveal to us the origin and beginnings of the Nation of Israel, and in the first eleven chapters we are shown the different steps by which Israel became a separate and Divinely chosen nation."

Wise old Solomon stated: *"That which has been is that which will be, and that which has been done is that which will be done. So there is nothing new under the sun." (Ecclesiastes 1:9)* One of my great delights over the past number of years has been the privilege of teaching at several Bible Schools or Colleges. While speaking on "The Qualifications For Kings and Priests," I've often mentioned my longstanding desire to write a book with the title *The Gentile Roots Of The Jewish Faith.* Recently I taught at The Bible College of Wales and once again mentioned this possibility. Following my class, one of the students encouraged me to begin writing. This wasn't the first such encouragement; our daughter Lisa has urged me on several occasions, and God also seemed to be leading me in this direction. The other day I was prayed over by several people, one of whom said they felt the Lord wanted me to continue writing.

Those who know me realize that writing is not my first love—far from it. If not for proofreaders and editors, my books would never see the light of day. However, I love God's Word and I believe He's given me insight that will encourage you to explore these truths for yourself. Therefore, I have continued writing. I hope that, by the time it's in your hands, this book will not only be inspirational and applicable to your Christian life, but also *readable*.

ONE

The Law of Beginnings

Many old time expositors referred to what they called *The Law of Beginnings* or *The Law of First Mention*—meaning the first time a word or phrase appears in the Bible, *how* it's used often provides great insight into its meaning throughout the rest of the Scriptures.

G.D. Watson describes this in his book *God's First Words*: "*The book of Genesis contains God's first words in His revelation to the human race, and these first words are the pattern and sample of all other words in the Bible. I discovered some years ago that every doctrine that is taught in the Scripture is first mentioned or referred to in the book of Genesis, and that this wonderful book is the seed bed of every growth in the entire scope of divine revelation.*

"As we go through the Bible we find that the first words contained in Genesis are enlarged and unfolded in a great many different directions and applications, but the words themselves are never changed and they are never any more perfect in the last book of the Bible than they are in the first. God's words never need any correction or any improvement, but only to be unfolded and applied as time and generations go by." (God's First Words *by G .D. Watson Published by Harvey and Tait, Hampton, TN 37658)*

The first three mentions in Genesis of the word "heart" illustrate this truth. The word appears hundreds of times in Scripture, but what exactly does it refer to? Genesis Chapter Six, verse five reads: *"Then God saw that the wickedness of man was great on the earth, and every intent of the thoughts of his heart was only evil continually."* Here the word *heart* refers to man's THINKING or THOUGHTS. Verse six states: *"And the Lord was sorry that he had made man on the earth, and He was grieved in His heart."* Here *heart* refers to the EMOTIONS. The word *heart* next appears in Chapter Eight, verse twenty-one: *"And the Lord smelled the soothing aroma; and the Lord said in His heart, I will never again curse the ground on account of man, for the intent of man's heart is evil from his youth . . ."* Here the word *heart* refers to the WILL. These first three references give a clear understanding of how the word is used throughout the Bible. When Scripture speaks of a *divided heart* or says *unite my heart* or *give me your heart*, it refers to man's MIND, WILL and EMOTIONS.

Consider also the usage of the word "flesh." This word is first found in Genesis Chapter Six, verse three: *"Then the Lord said, My Spirit shall not strive with men forever, because he also is flesh . . ."'* The margin of the NASB reads: " . . . in his going astray he is flesh." So *flesh* describes man's tendency to do his own thing or to stray from God's purpose.

Another example of the importance of understanding the beginning of a matter is the question posed to Jesus, by the Jews, concerning the matter of divorce. Seeking to back up their argument by quoting Moses, they no doubt expected to finally back Jesus into a corner and declare themselves the debate champions. However, Jesus' answer silenced them and revealed God's original intent regarding marriage: *"Because of your hardness of heart, Moses permitted you to divorce your wives; but from the **beginning** it has not been this way." (Matthew 19:8)* [Emphasis mine.]

Genesis is full of *seed truths*—firsts and beginnings. It contains the first marriage, first tabernacle, first sin, first discipline, first sacrifice, etc. With the *Law of First Mention* in mind, let's explore the fascinating book of beginnings, Genesis.

TWO

The First Tabernacle

I won't be delving into the "Gap theory" or the belief that there was a *creation* prior to the present one. Whether the world is millions or billions of years old is of no real concern to this writer. God is well capable of making something with *vintage* even though newly created. Take the case of Jesus turning water into wine. Although the wine had just been created, it had to be *aged* in order to be wine. Do you see my point?

As we begin our journey we'll weave in various Scriptural references to gain understanding of our topic — *Gentile roots*. In my library are a number of books about the Tabernacle of Moses, David's Tabernacle, and Solomon's Temple. Having spent some fifteen years of my ministry in New Zealand, I was well acquainted with the rich teachings

surrounding the various dwelling places of God —
due in part to the *Brethren Movement* in that country
years ago. It laid a strong biblical foundation for this
topic. However, I had never heard anyone refer to
God's *first* dwelling place. That changed when, by
chance, I picked up an old book by Robert Govett
M.A. titled, *The New Jerusalem,* written around 1874.
Charles Spurgeon said of Govett, "His works will
be worth their weight in gold one day." That's quite
an accolade coming from a preacher who many call
"The Prince of Preachers."

Govett writes, "After the creation of the world
in general, the Most High singled out a special
spot in the land of Eden in which He prepared a
garden for the abode of Adam." Govett refers to
this as the *first* tabernacle. This may seem a bit of
a stretch to the casual reader, but here we discover
(or uncover) some interesting facts. Here's how
Richard Davidson from Andrews University
supports this: "There is an emerging consensus
among biblical scholars that the pre-Fall Garden
of Eden (and its surroundings) is to be regarded as
the original sanctuary on earth, a copy of the sanc-
tuary/temple in heaven. The biblical evidence for
this conclusion has been documented by scores of
biblical scholars . . ."

In Genesis Chapter Two, verse eight, we read:
*"And the Lord planted a garden toward the east in
Eden."* The word "planted" (according to *Wilson's
Old Testament Word Studies*) means: *to plant, settle,*

*establish (a people); to drive in a nail, to set up an image;
to pitch or erect a tent, from the driving in of the tent pin*
. . . The word "garden" means: *to cover, cover over,
surround, defend or enclose.* Imagine God erecting a
tent by driving in tent pegs to form an enclosure
or covering. This garden—or enclosure—brings to
mind the Tabernacle of Moses, or (prior to that) the
Tent of Meeting. In the very beginning God drove in
tent pegs and formed a covering. This became not
only God's dwelling place, but also the dwelling
place of Adam and Eve.

This enclosure became the place of God's presence, the original Tent of Meeting. We could also say
that this was God's command center from which
man was to receive God's mind as it pertained to
subduing the earth. Some may ask, *But wasn't this
a real garden with trees and flowers etc?* No doubt this
tabernacle was much more than a small confined
place like that of Moses Tabernacle or Solomon's
Temple. It was instead a large expanse in which to
live, work, and (more importantly) fellowship with
God. After all, this was God's abode that Adam and
Eve were privileged to dwell in.

When Moses was told to make the lampstand,
its design was like an almond tree with branches
containing cups shaped like almond blossoms.
Solomon, likewise, decorated the inside of the
Temple with carvings of cherubim, palm trees, and
open flowers. These were mans attempt to copy or
create a garden—like the first tabernacle made by

God. Since man is incapable of creating real flowers and palm trees, he carves their likeness instead.

When God told Moses to construct the tabernacle, He said, *"And let them construct a sanctuary for Me, that I may dwell among them."* *(Exodus 25:8)* The ultimate purpose behind the tabernacle was God's longing to be with His people. The Apostle Paul reminds us, in his letter to the Colossians, that Christ is *"to have first place in everything."* *(Colossians 1:18)* This is borne out by the statement in Genesis 2:9 that the tree of life was *"in the midst"* of the garden—this is the same term for the living presence of God *"in the midst"* of His people in the sanctuary, in the Tabernacle of Moses, and in Solomon's Temple, where the ark symbolizes the presence of God. This is all beautifully illustrated by God's creation of the *garden*. Govett writes: "The plan of God, as originally sketched at creation, was marred by the sin of Satan and of man. But it was not abandoned. Ever since that day, the Lord has been working to re-establish Eden on a basis not to be shaken. His end shall certainly be attained at last, with the ruin of all who attempt to resist it."

God created this garden as His earthly dwelling place, His command center, or Kingdom headquarters. I can only imagine how glorious this garden was; after all, " . . . *in His presence is fullness of joy and at His right hand are pleasure forevermore."* From this garden paradise, man was to go forth and subdue the earth. This reminds me of Jesus' words: *"I will build My church [His earthly dwelling place] and the gates of hell will not prevail against it."* From the beginning God intended His people to rule and reign. I'll have more to say about this later—first we must return to Eden and explore the significance of the river which flowed from it.

THREE

The First River or Laver

We read in Genesis that God created a river to flow from Eden. In both the natural and spiritual sense, rivers speak of *life*. Without water, life is impossible. The river flowing from Eden eventually became four rivers, bringing life wherever it flowed. Richard Davidson, in his book *Earth's First Sanctuary*, writes this about the river: "The Genesis 2 creation account implies that the Garden of Eden was placed on an elevated position, i. e., a mountain: the four rivers flow from a common source in four different directions (Genesis 2:10-14), and this seems possible only if rivers are flowing down from an elevated (mountain) location." Robert Govett elaborates on this when he states, "Eden was created by God; the tabernacle was made by man. Hence the inferiority of the creature's power must be manifest. God can, and does, make the *river*, with its perpetual motion. Man cannot do this. His imitation of a river can be only a vessel containing water. Such was the *laver* of the tabernacle."

The laver was where the priests were washed before entering the priestly service. Following this washing, they were clothed in their priestly attire. This task was done for them in Exodus 29:4. Following this initial washing (that never needed to be repeated), they were required to wash daily before entering into the Holy Place or *Holy of Holies*. "*And the Lord spoke to Moses, saying, You shall also make a laver of bronze, with its base of bronze for washing; and you shall put it between the tent of meeting and the altar, and you shall put water in it. And Aaron and his sons shall wash their hands and their feet from it; when they enter the tent of meeting, they shall wash with water, that they may not die . . .*" *(Exodus 30:17-20.)*

I could elaborate on this in detail, but the laver was simply man's attempt to make a *river*. No doubt the river that flowed from Eden supplied the daily needs of Adam and Eve both for washing and refreshment. When we study *all* of the dwelling places created by God, we see that they don't have *lavers*, but rather *rivers* flowing from them. Ezekiel describes God's house in Ezekiel Chapter Forty-Seven: "*Then he brought me back to the door of the house; and behold water was flowing from under the threshold of the house toward the east, for the house faced east. And the water was flowing down from under, the right side of the house . . . and he led me through the water, water reaching the ankles . . . water reaching the knees . . . water reaching the loins . . . water to swim in, a river that could not be forded . . . so everything will live where the river goes."*

Isaiah also describes a river flowing from God's presence, broad enough for boats. Here is what he describes: *"Look upon Zion, the city of our appointed feasts; your eyes will see Jerusalem an undisturbed habitation, a tent which shall not be folded, its stakes shall never be pulled up nor any of its cords torn apart. But there the Majestic One, the Lord, shall be for us a place of rivers and wide canals on which no boat with oars shall go, and on which no mighty ship shall pass."* (Isaiah 33:20-21)

In John's Revelation we read in Chapter Twenty-Two, verse one: *"And he showed me a river of the water of life, clear as crystal, coming from the throne of God and of the Lamb."* As God's redeemed *temples*, we also are to have a *river of life* flowing from us. *"Now on the last day, the great day of the feast, Jesus stood and cried out, saying, 'If any man is thirsty, let him come to Me and drink. He who believes in Me, as the Scripture said, "From his innermost being shall flow rivers of living water."' But this He spoke of the Spirit . . ."* (John 7:37-39) Jesus said this is only possible after we've been filled with the Spirit of God.

Without being filled with the Holy Spirit we are inadequate and incapable of producing a river of life—our spiritual womb is closed. The word *womb* is the literal meaning of the word translated as *belly* or innermost being. No doubt the various translators sought to use a more generic word, as *womb* is gender specific. The womb is the place of conception and birth. Only the Spirit of God can open our barren spiritual wombs and cause a river of life to flow forth.

Return now to our study of the first tabernacle where we see God's original plan for man: God created man for fellowship with Himself. Every day God walked and talked with Adam and Eve. They strolled together among the trees and flowers of His garden. This was God's earthly home and His tent of meeting for His children. The Garden of Eden faced the east, and that was true of every one of God's dwelling places—including Moses' Tabernacle, Solomon's Temple and Ezekiel's Temple. They were positioned to catch the first light of dawn each new day. As God's temples, we too are to be children of the light, not of darkness. The Psalmist understood this principle of beginning the day seeking after God when he penned the words: *"O God, thou art my God; **early will I seek thee**: my soul thirsteth for thee, my flesh longeth for thee in a dry and thirsty land, where no water is . . ."* (Psalm 63:1, KJV) [Emphasis mine.] In Matthew we're also reminded that Jesus will return from the *east*. *"For just as the lightning comes from the east, and flashes even to the west, so shall the coming of the Son of Man be."* (Matthew 24:27)

I'd like to return to the *purpose* of the garden again. As I've already stated, Genesis is the book of beginnings, and therefore it gives us insight into God's original plan and purpose for man. Understanding the beginning of things is vital if we want to understand God's intent. In the next chapter we'll look into God's desire for fellowship with His children.

FOUR

The First Priests

The first picture of God's relationship with man is found in Chapter One, verse twenty-eight. Here we're told that before God commissioned man to be fruitful and replenish the earth, He *blessed* them. The Hebrew word used here means to *kneel down and bless.* What a beautiful illustration — God the Father kneeling (as it were) over His children, and no doubt laying His hands upon them to impart His blessing. Some two thousand years later God spoke to Moses saying, *"Speak to Aaron and to his sons, saying 'Thus you shall bless the sons of Israel. You shall say to them: The Lord bless you, and keep you; the Lord make His face to shine on you, and be gracious to you; the Lord lift up His countenance on you, and give you peace.'" (Numbers 6:23-26)*

Following God's blessing, man was instructed to multiply and replenish the earth. Thinking in natural terms, we assume God just wanted the earth populated. However, there's more going on in the mind of God than just that. Originally, man was created in God's image and expressed a measure of God's glory. After all, we're told that as a result of sin we *fall short of the glory of God*. God's intention (before the fall) was to fill the earth with *His glory*. We're reminded again of this when, following Moses' intercession on behalf of Israel after they created and worshipped the golden calf, we read: *"So the Lord said, I have pardoned them according to your word; but indeed, as I live, all the earth will be filled with the glory of the Lord." (Numbers 14:20-21)*

Incidentally, when I mention the glory of God, I'm not necessarily referring to some bright shimmering light display, but rather the very nature and character of God. When Jesus performed His first miracle by turning water into wine, we read that He *manifested His glory*. God's deep longing from the start has been to have people who will reveal His character and nature. This longing will one day be realized through His glorious church having no spot or wrinkle.

After blessing Adam and Eve, God placed them in the garden to cultivate and keep it. We've already seen that this was much more than a picket fence surrounding some trees and a flowerbed. It was the very dwelling place of God. Adam and

Eve were to *cultivate* and *keep* this garden. These same words are translated elsewhere as "serve" and "guard" — they appear together in connection with Moses' tabernacle. The job of the priest was to serve and guard the tabernacle. God told Moses to bring the sons of Aaron and anoint them to serve as priests. *"They shall also keep all the furnishings of the tent of meeting, along with the duties of the sons of Israel, to do the service of the tabernacle." (Numbers 3:8)* The words *keep* and *service* have the same root (or meaning) as *cultivate* and *keep,* which God used when He spoke to Adam and Eve. Again, in First Chronicles Twenty-Three, verse thirty-two, the words are used: *"Thus they are to keep charge of the tent of meeting, and charge of the holy place, and charge of the sons of Aaron their relative, for the service [same root as* cultivate*] of the house of the Lord."*

Not only did Adam and Eve serve in the garden, but they fellowshipped with their Creator. In the cool of the day His presence filled the garden as He walked before them. This picture of God *walking among them* is identical with what we find in Deuteronomy Twenty-Three, verse fourteen: *"Since the Lord your God walks in the midst of your camp . . ."* and again in Leviticus Twenty Six, verse eleven and twelve: *"Moreover, I will make My dwelling among you, and My soul will not reject you. I will also walk among you and be your God, and you shall be My people."*

We're not told how long Adam and Eve walked with God. Perhaps it was many years, like Enoch after them. Because we tend to read over these verses quickly, we miss the time element. We assume man fell almost immediately, but that is obviously not the case. Even the time Adam would have needed to study and name each animal couldn't have been accomplished overnight.

In our study of the first tabernacle, we see a twofold function (or calling) given to Adam and Eve: that of *kings* and *priests*. As kings they received authority to subdue the earth. As priests they had the high calling of worship and fellowship with God. We must keep in mind that the highest function of a priest wasn't his relationship to the people, but rather to God Himself. This is clearly illustrated in Ezekiel Forty-Four where we see two categories of priests. The first group of priests went astray after idols, so they were banned from ministering directly to the Lord. However, they were allowed to function as priests on behalf of the people — presenting the various offerings brought to them by the people. God declared that they were not permitted to *"come near to Me to minister as priests."* We read about the second group in verse fifteen: *"But the Levitical priests, the sons of Zadok who kept charge of My sanctuary when the sons of Israel went astray from Me, shall come near to Me to minister to Me; and they shall stand before Me to offer Me the fat and the blood, declares the Lord God."*

Notice that the priests who went astray were given the largest audience. They ministered to the entire nation. But those who remained faithful were given the higher honor — they ministered to God Himself. For those who moan about not having some type of public ministry, remember the greater calling is to minister to *Him*.

If you're familiar with God's Word, you know that a two-fold theme of kings and priests runs throughout the Bible. We are indeed a *royal priesthood*. Some expositors see a three-fold division in these opening chapters of Genesis, similar to the threefold division of the tabernacle. The tabernacle contained three distinct areas, including the outer court, the Holy place and the Holy of Holies. Likewise, Genesis has a threefold division: the world, Eden, and the garden. Much more could be said regarding this, but for now we'll move on.

FIVE

The First King and Kingdom

Jesus taught us to pray, *"Thy Kingdom come, Thy will be done, on earth as it is in heaven . . ."* Do you think this thought first entered God's mind at that exact moment? I don't think so. I believe this was God's intention from the beginning.

God told Israel, *"The Lord has today declared you to be His people, a treasured possession, as He promised you, and that you should keep His commandments; and that He shall set you high above all nations which He has made, for praise, fame, and honor; and that you shall be a consecrated people to the Lord your God, as He has spoken."* In the following chapter of Deuteronomy, Israel was again told by God, *" . . . you shall lend to many nations, but you shall not borrow. And the Lord shall make you the head and not the tail, and you only shall be above, and you shall not be underneath . . ."* (Deuteronomy 26:18-19, 28:12-13)

Long before God gave that promise to Israel, He had in mind a people who would rule and take dominion. No sooner had He created man than He gave him His commission: " . . . *and let them rule over the fish of the sea and over the birds of the sky and over the cattle and over all the earth, and over every creeping thing that creeps on the earth . . . and fill the earth and subdue it; and rule over . . . every living thing that moves on the earth."* (Genesis 1:26, 28)

When God created man in His image, what was that image? When Philip desired to see the Father, Jesus replied, *"Philip, He who has seen Me has seen the Father." (John 14:9)* The *image of God* is the Lord Jesus Christ—the King of kings and Lord of lords. Since man was created in God's image, it stands to reason that he has also been given authority and dominion.

In his book *God's First Words*, G. D. Watson states: "Everything that God does is according to some pattern which exists in the divine mind. Hence, when He arranged the creation of the world, and man, He formed a plan of the kingdom which He would set up on this earth, of which Adam and Eve were to be the co-regents over all the lower creation, and that they should bring forth a race of rulers that should have dominion over the material universe . . . the same idea was expressed just after the flood, when Noah and his family came out of the ark, when God said to Noah, 'Be fruitful, and multiply, and replenish the earth. And the fear of you shall be upon every beast of the earth, and upon every fowl of the air, upon all that moveth upon the earth . . . into your hand are they delivered.'"

We know from Psalm Eight that this same concept was revealed to the Psalmist: *"What is man, that Thou dost take thought of him, and the son of man that Thou dost care for him? Yet Thou hast made him a little lower than God, and hast crowned him with glory and majesty! Thou dost make him to rule over the works of Thy hands; and hast put all things under his feet, all sheep and oxen and also the beasts of the field, the birds of the heavens, and the fish of the sea, whatever passes through the paths of the seas." (Psalm 8:4-8, KJV)*

God intended man to rule, yet man fell far short of God's intention. However, God continued seeking a people who would exercise their God-given calling and commission. As we've read, this purpose was passed on to Israel. G. Campbell Morgan provides amazing insight regarding this: "It cannot be too often emphasized that it was not the election of a nation from among others in order that upon that nation God might lavish His love while He abandoned the others. The purpose of God was far wider than that of the creation of this nation; it was that of the creation of a testimony, for the sake of the others. The Divine intention was the creation of a people who, under His divine government, should reveal in the world the breath and beauty and beneficence of that government; a people who gathered in their national life about His throne and His altar, obeying His commands and worshipping Him, should reveal to outside nations the meaning of the Kingdom of God. It was not the selection of a pet, but the creation of a pattern." *(Living Messages of the Books of the Bible; Fleming H. Revell Company; page 32.)*

This was God's intention for Adam and Eve. As priests they had access to God's first tabernacle, an opportunity to enjoy intimate fellowship with their Creator and then, in turn, to express their love to Him through adoration and worship. As kings they were to go forth and conqueror. This theme of *kings* and *priests* runs throughout God's word.

In the New Testament, *church* is the word "Ekklesia." In his book *New Testament Words,* William Barclay gives us insight into the Greek background of the word: "In the great classical days in Athens, the *ekklesia* was the convened assembly of the people. It consisted of all the citizens of the city who had not lost their civic rights. Apart from the fact that its decisions must conform to the laws of the State, its powers were (to all intents and purposes) unlimited. It elected and dismissed magistrates and directed the policy of the city. It declared war, made peace, contracted treaties and arranged alliances. It elected generals and other military officers . . . It was ultimately responsible for the conduct of all military operations."

Clearly, Jesus had something greater in mind for his church than Easter egg hunts, rummage sales, and other fundraisers. Jesus intended to have a people who would *turn the world upside-down* — against whom *the gates of hell* were no match.

Allow me to quote from Charles H. Spurgeon on this. 'Hath He not said,"I will dwell in them and walk in them"? And it is out of the church, the spiritual palace of God, that His glory shines forth among men. The promise of the hundred and tenth psalm is, "The Lord shall send forth the rod of thy strength out of Zion; rule in the misdt of thine enemies." I you desire to see God's spiritual power you will discern it best by seeing how it is exerted in and through spiritual men and spiritual women, built up together as a spiritual house. The church of Christ is the camp from which the armies of the Lord go forth to conquer the nations; it is the pavilion in which the Prince of Peace has fixed his head-quarters during this last crusade. If you ask for the center of the nations, if you would discover the eye and soul of this poor world, if you would fain see the glory and excellence of the sons of men, find out the quickened stones that God hath builded together, and you will see the habitation of the great King.' *(Taken from page 547. Volume 23. Metropolitian Tabernacle Pulpit. Pilgrim Publications, Pasadena, Texas. 1979)*

SIX

The First Sin

If you've read my book *Blood Bought*, you're familiar with my theory that *the fall of Satan* and *the fall of man* occurred almost simultaneously. The following verses helped lead me to that conclusion: If Ezekiel's account in Chapter Twenty-Eight (regarding the King of Tyre) refers to Lucifer, as most expositors believe, then we're told, beginning in verse thirteen, *"You were in Eden the garden of God; every precious stone was your covering; the ruby, the topaz, and the diamond; the beryl, the onyx, and the jasper; the lapis lazuli, the turquoise, and the emerald . . . you were the anointed cherub that covers . . . you were on the holy mountain of God."*

Let's take these statements apart and examine them one-by-one, beginning with the last:

"You were on the holy mountain of God." As I've previously stated, most (if not all) of God's dwellings were situated on mountains. We can safely assume that when God drove in those nails or tent pegs to form His garden, He chose a mountain—thereby establishing a *pattern* or *type*. When God brought the children of Israel out of Egypt, we read: " . . . *until the people pass over whom Thou hast purchased. Thou wilt bring them and plant them in the mountain of Thine inheritance, the place, O Lord, which Thou hast made for Thy dwelling." (Exodus 15:17, KJV)* Mountains are known to be a source for rivers; hence the river that flowed out from Eden. Ezekiel also refers to Lucifer as the *"anointed cherub who covers or guards."* Cherubim were an intricate part of the tabernacle or temple; we see them covering the ark, on the veil of the tabernacle and on the walls of the temple etc. From these details we understand that this was no ordinary garden, but rather a type of holy sanctuary—a dwelling place for the most High.

Now for the real clincher: *"You were in Eden, the garden of God."* Ezekiel refers to Lucifer in his previous state, before his fall. To the best of my knowledge, we have no record of *heaven* being referred to as *"Eden, the garden of God."* Finally, we read of Lucifer: " . . . *every precious stone was your covering; the ruby, the topaz, and the diamond; the beryl, the onyx, and the jasper; the lapis lazuli, the turquoise, and the emerald."* This description immediately reminds me of the High Priest wearing the breast-plate of various stones—each representing the tribes of Israel. Many of the stones listed here, with Lucifer, remind us of the priestly service associated with the tabernacle and temple.

But what caused this anointed cherub to be referred to as "you were"? Some cataclysmic event took place that caused Satan to *"fall from heaven like lightning." (Luke 10:18)* To trace this event, we return to the beginning. Following the creation of each of the seven days, God declared them good. Never once does God say, "Except for Satan; he's evil!" Following the creation of Adam and Eve, after their placement in the garden, God does not tell them to avoid the serpent. Why not? Throughout God's word, He warns us about our adversary, the devil, telling us not to be ignorant of his devices. So why on earth didn't God warn His children about this tempter, seducer, beguiler, deceiver, and liar—the devil—at the beginning? To me, this alone is proof that Lucifer had not yet fallen and was still the anointed cherub.

Keep in mind that man was originally a spiritual being. As someone recently explained, we are "a spirit, with a soul, which dwells in a body." Apparently, man became *self-conscious* after the fall, as he saw his nakedness and sought to hide from God. Before this, man appeared *spirit conscious*—happily content to spend time in fellowship with God. Forget the idea that Adam and Eve spent their days pruning roses and weeding out the vegetable patch. The garden was God's sanctuary, His earthly dwelling place and the place of His presence. Here He delighted to spend time with His family. Listen to Solomon's poetic declaration in Proverbs Chapter Eight, verse thirty and thirty one: *"Then I was beside Him, as a master workman; I was daily His delight, Rejoicing always before Him, rejoicing in the world, His earth, and having my delight in the sons of men."* God delighted in His sons.

Every parent knows the joy of welcoming home their newborn. How much more do you think God delights in His vast family of sons and daughters? The prophet Zephaniah reminds us that, *"The Lord our God is in your midst, a victorious warrior. He will exult over you with joy, he will renew you in His love, He will rejoice over you with shouts of joy."* If God does this over His fallen creation, I can only wonder what it must have been like in the beginning, when sin had not defiled the earth as it has now. No doubt, the garden was a literal paradise in every sense of that word. In Psalm Sixteen, verse eleven, we're reminded: *"In Thy presence is fullness of joy; in Thy right hand there are pleasures forevermore."* We quickly pass over Genesis Two without musing or meditating on what it must have been like to be *in the presence of the Almighty* — to know and experience the pleasure of His company. Just writing about this creates in me a longing to be in His eternal presence. What a blessed hope awaits us!

From our understanding so far, we can conclude that Lucifer played an important and vital role in God's earthly sanctuary. I believe that as the months and years — perhaps even decades — passed, Lucifer saw Adam and Eve's relationship with God develop more and more. Time with their Maker was the highlight of their day. But Lucifer was jealous of the worship and attention he saw being lavished upon God by His children. Lucifer was *"full of wisdom and beauty."* He craved recognition and adulation for his role as the covering cherub. James tells us, *" . . . each one is tempted when he is carried away and enticed by his own lust. Then when lust has conceived, it gives birth to sin; and when sin is accomplished, it brings forth death."* (James 1:14-15) Perhaps it was at this stage that Lucifer said, *"I will ascend to heaven [God's throne]; I will raise my throne above the stars of God, and I will sit on the mount of the assembly in the recesses of the north. I will ascend above the heights of the clouds; I will make myself like the Most High."* (Isaiah 14:13-14) I believe this is when one of the most cataclysmic events in all history took place — a seraph became a serpent, and the devil emerged as the *"Father of Lies."* (John 8:44)

What convinced me that this scenario wasn't only probable, but also entirely possible, was the confrontation between God and the serpent, following Adam's sin in eating the forbidden fruit. Adam blamed Eve, and Eve, in turn, blamed the serpent. Then we read: *"And the Lord said to the serpent, because you have done this, cursed are you more than all cattle, and more than every beast of the field; on your belly shall you go, and dust shall you eat all the days of your life; and I will put enmity between you and the woman, and between your seed and her seed: He shall bruise you on the head and you shall bruise him on the heel." (Genesis 3:14-15)* These two verses are extremely important for understanding Satan's fall. First of all, God said, *"Because you have done this, cursed are you"* – in other words, prior to this, the serpent wasn't cursed. This was God's sentence for the serpent's sin. We're never told of any curse placed on the serpent before this. Unfortunately, we tend to assume that the serpent was already corrupt when we read in Genesis Three, verse one, *"Now the serpent was more crafty than any beast of the field . . ."* The word *crafty* makes us think he's evil. But the word used here (translated as *crafty*) is sometimes translated as *prudent*, which has a positive connotation.

Returning to God's judgment on the serpent, we read, *"On your belly shall you go, and dust shall you eat all the days of your life."* Obviously, the serpent wasn't on his belly eating dust prior to this. Now for the real proof that this was a simultaneous fall: God continued to say, *"And I will put enmity between you and the woman . . ."* This statement alone reveals that there was *no enmity* between the serpent and Adam and Eve before this day. This is why God never warned Adam and Eve about the serpent – they were not *enemies* prior to this.

The serpent's action caused him to be cast down, as we read in Ezekiel Chapter Twenty-Eight, verse sixteen: " . . . *and you sinned; Therefore I have cast you as profane from the mountain of God. And I have destroyed you, O covering cherub."* Now we see why Paul wrote to Timothy: *"For it was Adam who was first created, and then Eve, and it was not Adam who was deceived, but the woman, being quite deceived, fell into transgression." (1 Timothy 2:14-15)* This deception wasn't readily apparent. As I've stated, months, years, and maybe decades may have passed before the fall. During this time, the anointed cherub became a trusted friend. After all, God had placed him in the garden and clothed him with the perfection of beauty. No doubt the three of them spent countless hours, days, months or years together. Eve had no reason to doubt his words if he was a trusted friend. Just as Jesus was betrayed in the house of His friends, here too a trusted friend might have turned against the very one he was meant to guard. We might also conclude that God's own son and daughter were deceived into betraying their own Creator and faithful Friend.

Although this passage exposes one of the saddest days in earth's history, it also provides us with the greatest promise. We read in verse fifteen of Genesis Three, *"He shall bruise you on the head and you shall bruise him on the heel."* What a priceless promise God gave for Adam's offspring. In these verses we find not only the root of man's sin, but also the hope of his redemption – as we'll read about in the next chapter.

(For a complete understanding of the meaning of *redemption,* read my book *Blood Bought.*)

SEVEN

The First Messianic Promise

In the last chapter we explored Lucifer's fall and sin's entrance into the world. Now we'll read about the glorious promise of a coming Redeemer – God's promised *seed* who would crush the serpent's head.

Herbert Lockyer writes: "The only key to all Messianic prophecy is found hanging at the front door of the Bible, and, strange though it may be, this key was given by God to that 'old serpent, the devil.' He was the first to learn of a Deliverer who would come to destroy his devilish works. To him was given the initial promise and prophecy of redemption from the sin he had brought into God's fair universe."

Arthur W. Pink, in his exposition of Genesis, goes much deeper: *"'We love Him because He first loved us.'"* O, that we might appreciate more deeply the marvelous condescension of Deity in stooping so low as to care for and seek out such poor worms of the dust. *'And I will put enmity between thee and the woman, and between thy seed and her seed; it shall bruise thy head, and thou shalt bruise his heel.' (Genesis 3:15)* Here again we behold the exceeding riches of God's grace. Before He acted in judgment, He displayed mercy; before He banished the guilty ones from Eden, He gave them a blessed promise and hope. Though Satan had encompassed the downfall of man, it's announced that One shall come and bruise his head. By woman had come sin; by woman should come the Savior. By woman had come the curse, by woman should come Him who would bear and remove the curse. By woman Paradise was lost, yet by woman should be born the One who should regain it. O what grace – the Lord of glory was to be the *woman's* seed! Here we have the beginning and germ of all prophecy." *(Gleanings in Genesis, Arthur W. Pink; Moody Press, page 42.)*

Davidson states it this way: "The Messiah would volunteer to consciously step on the head of the most deadly viper in the universe, the serpent Satan himself, knowing full well that it would cost him his life. For many Christians, this is a powerful portrait of the substitutionary sacrifice of Christ on our behalf." *(Page 75, Earth's First Sanctuary.)*

God spoke this amazing Messianic promise long before man acknowledged his sin or his need of a Savior — what a marvelous revelation of God's nature and character! I'm reminded of the writer of Hebrews when he addressed the fulfillment of this promise: *"Since the children share in flesh and blood, He Himself likewise also partook of the same, that through death He might render powerless him that had the power of death, that is the devil; and might deliver those who through fear of death were subject to slavery all their lives." (Hebrews 2:14-15)*

The hymn writer Charles Wesley expressed it well in his Christmas carol, "Hark the Herald Angels Sing."

> *Come, Desire of nations, come!*
> *Fix in us Thy humble home:*
> *Rise, the woman's conqu'ring seed,*
> *Bruise in us the serpent's head;*
> *Adam's likeness now efface,*
> *Stamp Thine image in its place:*
> *Final Adam from above,*
> *Reinstate us in Thy love.*

EIGHT

The First Sacrifice

In this chapter we'll look at the first sacrifice for sin – which came long before God gave Israel instructions regarding the sin offering and other sacrifices. Following man's first sin we read this: *"The Lord God made garments of skin for Adam and his wife, and clothed them."* (Genesis 3:21)

God had warned Adam and Eve that if they ate of the tree of the knowledge of good and evil they would die. First would come spiritual death – in other words, being separated from fellowship with God. This would be followed by physical death. We know God is just and righteous in all His ways, and therefore sin had to be punished. However, not only is God *just*, but He's also *merciful*. Yet, if God shows only mercy, His justice will suffer. We read of King Darius facing this dilemma when his trusted friend Daniel was found guilty of breaking the king's decree not to pray to, or worship, any other god than *himself.* Daniel was thrown into the lion's den, and we're told the king set his mind on delivering Daniel. How could he show mercy to his trusted friend and counselor, while at the same time upholding his own law? Unable to reconcile the two, he said to Daniel, *"Your God, who you constantly serve, will Himself deliver you." (Daniel 6:16)*

God's answer to man's sin was to uphold His justice by providing a *substitute,* while at the same time extending mercy to the guilty. God took an innocent life in order to clothe man with its skin – here we have the gospel message first illustrated. The writer of Hebrews tells us: *"Without the shedding of blood there is no forgiveness of sin."* By this act, God provided a covering for man's sin – and it foreshadowed the death of Jesus Christ, *God's lamb.* God provided all that was necessary. Man needed only to accept; no payment was required from him. Isaiah reminds us: *"I will rejoice greatly in the Lord, my soul will exult in my God; for He has clothed me with garments of salvation, He has wrapped me with a robe of righteousness . . ." (Isaiah 61:10)*

God's provision of a substitute (to cover man's sin and shame) speaks of God's love. *"But God demonstrates His own love toward us, in that while we were yet sinners, Christ died for us." (Romans 5:8)* As the old hymn writer expressed it:

Nothing in my hand I bring,
Simply to thy cross I cling;
Naked, come to thee for dress,
Helpless, look to thee for grace;
Foul, I to the Fountain fly;
Wash me, Savior, or I die.

We don't read of Adam and Eve seeking a covering from God; instead we see God taking the first step in providing a covering for them. What an amazing God we have, who (long before we sought salvation) had already provided a sacrifice, that we could be saved. Like the Prodigal of old, all that's required of us is that we turn from our sin and return to the Father. The Father's love caused Him to run and embrace His wayward son, smothering him in kisses, then providing him with the best robe, shoes and ring. No wonder the writer to the Hebrews refers to our salvation as *"so great a salvation."* *(Hebrews 2:3)* The hymn writer Fanny Crosby expressed it this way in 1875:

To God Be the Glory

To God be the glory, great things He hath done;
So loved He the world that He gave us His Son,
Who yielded His life an atonement for sin,
And opened the life gate that all may go in.

Praise the Lord, praise the Lord,
Let the earth hear His voice!
Praise the Lord, praise the Lord, Let the people rejoice!
O come to the Father, through Jesus the Son,
And give Him the glory, great things He hath done.

O perfect redemption, the purchase of blood,
To every believer the promise of God;
The vilest offender who truly believes,
That moment from Jesus a pardon receives.

Great things He hath taught us,
great things He hath done,
And great our rejoicing through Jesus the Son;
But purer, and higher, and greater will be
Our wonder, our rapture, when Jesus we see.

I came across an interesting fact regarding the word "clothed," that we see in Genesis 3:21. This very word is used to describe the covering, or clothing, of the priest, and it implies a change of status bestowed by God upon a priest. What an awesome thought, that God Almighty — through the sacrifice of His only Son, the Lord Jesus Christ — has made provision for us to be clothed in His righteousness and restored to His plan and purpose for our lives.

Robert S. Candlish, in his exposition *Studies in Genesis,* writes: "No Israelite living under the dispensation of Moses, when reading the account of God's clothing our first parents with skins, and afterwards accepting Abel's offering of a lamb, could have a moment's hesitation in concluding that, from the beginning, the sacrificial institute formed an essential part of the service which God required of fallen man ... Thus, to Jesus, The Seed of the woman, thou owest, O my guilty and enslaved souls, God's true liberty instead of Satan's lying bondage — prolonged life instead of instant death — and instead of the shame of thine own nakedness, the white raiment of the worthiness of the Lamb that was slain." *(Published by Kregel Publications, Grand Rapids, Michigan; page 84.)*

NINE

The First Discipline

Before discussing God's discipline of Adam and Eve, lets first return to God's intention for creating man. God said, *"Let us make man in our image . . ."* Some six thousand years after uttering those words, God's purpose for man remains the same. The Father longs to conform us to the image of His Son. The Apostle Paul tells us of Jesus the Son: *" . . . all things were created by Him and for Him."* *(Colossians 1:16)* God created us *for Himself*, to the praise of His glory. As John reminds us in Revelation Chapter Four, verse eleven: *" . . . for Thou didst create all things and because of Thy will they existed and were created."* The KJV translates it: *" . . . and for Thy plea- sure they are and were created."*

We must understand God's original plan and purpose for man, or we'll never really appreciate or understand God's redemptive purpose. The cross isn't just about God *cleansing* us. The cross is about God *claiming* us. As I've stated many times, "What the blood cleanses, it claims." To preach anything less than this is to deprive God of His claim on our life. Being conformed *to the image of God* remains God's intention for each of us. The new birth, as glorious as it may be, is just the beginning. Like newborn babes we're to desire the milk of the Word, that we might grow into His likeness. Like any parent, God rejoices over our new *birth in Christ*. Yet, if we remain spiritual infants, the Father's heart must break—an infant who fails to grow is often terminally ill.

John addresses three stages of growth in his First Epistle: *"I am writing to you little **children** . . . I'm writing to you **young men** . . . I am writing to you **fathers**."* (1 John 2:13) [Emphasis mine.] *Fathers* represents mature believers who have grown in Christ-likeness and who *"know Him who has been from the beginning."* These believers fully grasp God's intention, plan and purpose for man.

I wrote earlier that (before the fall) man was created to express the glory of God—meaning the nature of God. When I speak of the *glory of God* I'm not referring to a bright, pulsating halogen type of light—although Saul encountered something like that on the road to Damascus. I'm referring to God's nature and character. When Moses prayed, " . . . *show me Thy glory,"* God placed Moses on a rock, then said, *"My glory is passing by."* We then read: *"And the Lord descended in the cloud and stood there with him as he called upon the name of the Lord. Then the Lord passed by in front of him and proclaimed, 'The Lord God, compassionate and gracious, slow to anger, and abounding in loving-kindness and truth; who keeps loving-kindness for thousands, who forgives iniquity, transgression and sin; yet He will by no means leave the guilty unpunished, visiting the iniquity of the fathers on the children to the third and forth generations.'"* What a beautiful revelation of God's nature. It was this very nature that God intended man to express from the beginning.

Not only do we read of God's compassion, forgiveness, and graciousness etc., but also about God's punishment of the guilty. This brings us back to Adam and Eve and the consequences for their disobedience. Following their disobedience, they were driven out from the presence of God. *"So He drove the man out; and at the east of the Garden of Eden He stationed the cherubim, and the flaming sword which turned every direction, to guard the way to the tree of life."* (Genesis 3:24) We learn here that sin's *forgiveness* and sin's *consequences* are two entirely different matters. For example: If a man robs a bank and is later truly repentant, his repentance could lead to his forgiveness — but it will not remove his consequences. Although we're not told of Adam's repentance, it appears that clothing them in skins was an act of forgiveness on God's part. Also, while they were both forgiven, the consequences of their sin still came — they were driven from the garden.

Discipline reveals God's love. We're reminded in the letter to the Hebrews: *"For those whom the Lord loves He disciplines." (Hebrews 12:6)* Throughout the Old and New Testaments we read repeatedly of God's discipline in the lives of His people. Sadly, the church today shies away from this important truth — as do many parents. Discipline is not abuse; it's the outflow of genuine love. Hebrews reminds us, *"But if you are without discipline, of which all have become partakers, then you are illegitimate children and not sons." (Hebrews 12:8)* Israel was often instructed by God on how to administer discipline. This wasn't a one-size-fits-all approach, but rather specific discipline for specific sins — always with the motive *"to do good for you in the end." (Deuteronomy 8:16)*

Over the past number of years it's become increasing popular to hear worship leaders say, "God is good." In response the congregation responds, "All the time, God is good." This is certainly true, but there's a misconception that since God is good all the time, He must always be in a happy mood, and therefore never upset with us — no matter what we do. Nothing could be further from the truth. While God's love remains constant, His pleasure in us varies. God's discipline is motivated by His love for us and is designed to bring corrections to those areas of our life that God is not pleased with. My dear mother believed in the *laying on of hands.*

I don't ever recall singing, "Mother is good all the time. All the time Mother is good," while she was administering discipline to my naked posterior. Now I can thankfully look back with the full understanding that it was all *to do good for me in the end.* God never abuses His children, but He promises discipline if we disobey Him.

TEN

The First Altar

Following man's banishment from the garden, at the east of the Garden of Eden, God *"stationed the cherubim and the flaming sword, which turned every direction to guard the way to the tree of life." (Genesis 3:24)*

Let's read again from Robert Govett on this matter: "The Tabernacle of Moses, in general, represents Eden after the fall . . . The Mosaic Tabernacle was a building enclosed in a court, which was in size a hundred cubits by fifty. It was the dwelling place of the Creator, the God of Israel. It was a holy place, amidst an unholy people, though they were cleansed beyond the rest of the nations. They were fenced off from the House of God, and even from the court. Death was the penalty of their approach beyond the appointed limits." (Numbers 1:51; 3:10,38. 18:22) The one entrance to the tabernacle was from the east, as it was also in Eden... Cherubim were placed at the entrance of Eden; the cherubim were found also in the tabernacle of Moses.

"A sword of fire guarded against all entrance into the Garden. In the Mosaic tabernacle there was something answering thereto. Immediately fronting its door stood the altar of burnt offering, the fire of which was never to die out. The altar is of copper, which bears the fire better than iron. (Lev. 6:12) But the fire, then, does not prevent all entrance. It does not turn around to every point, as of old. It's fixed in one spot. It's not dangerous to those who may enter. The altar has found a substitute for the guilty, in the perfect sacrifice appointed of Jehovah. It feeds on the fat of the sacrifice. God smells therein a 'savor of rest.' It represents the justice of God; His eternal perfection."

The majority of expositors agree that the cherubim and flaming sword, which God stationed at the entrance to the garden, was the place where Cain and Abel brought their offerings. Govett states that this corresponds to the brazen altar we find at the entrance of Moses tabernacle. We're not told if Adam or his offspring ever gained access back into the garden. It appears they did not; God was concerned they would eat of the tree of life and live forever. How glorious then that, under the new covenant, we can enter the Holy Place with confidence—through the blood of our Redeemer, who rent the veil on our behalf.

It's important to consider that Noah, Abraham, Isaac and Jacob all made altars to God, long before Moses was instructed how the altar was to be made. In reading of these altars there's no mention of any elaborate structure of any type, which is in keeping with the details God later gave to Moses in Exodus: *"You shall make an altar of earth for Me, and you shall sacrifice on it your burnt offerings and your peace offerings, your sheep and your oxen; in every place where I will cause My name to be remembered. I will come to you and bless you. And if you make an altar of stones for Me, you shall not build it of cut stones, for if you wield your tool on it, you will profane it. And you shall not go up by steps to My altar, that your nakedness may not be exposed on it." (Exodus 20:24-26)*

Arthur W. Pink provides us with some valuable insight into the instructions God gave to Moses: "The first thing to notice about this altar is its extreme simplicity and plainness. This was in marked contrast from the 'gods of silver' and 'gods of gold v.23 of the heathen. The altar, which Israel was to erect unto God, must not be made of that which man had manufactured, nor beautified by his skill; there should be in it no excellence which human hand had imparted. Man would naturally suppose that an altar to be used for Divine sacrifices should be of gold, artistically designed and richly ornamented. Yes, but that would only allow man to glorify himself in his handiwork. The great God will allow 'no flesh' to glory in His presence." *(Gleanings In Exodus, page 167. Moody Press, Chicago.)*

We'll see later how Jacob took simple stones to erect an altar to God, long before God gave Moses these instructions. In our next chapter we'll look at the first offerings that man ever brought to God as we study the difference between Abel and Cain's offerings.

ELEVEN

The First Offerings or Tithe

Following man's expulsion from the garden, Cain and Abel brought offerings to the Lord. *"So it came about, in the course of time, that Cain brought an offering to the Lord of the fruit of the ground. And Abel, on his part, also brought of the firstlings of his flock and of their fat portions. And the Lord had regard for Abel and his offering; but for Cain and his offering He had no regard." (Genesis 4:3-4)* It appears that God had already established certain seasons in which His people were to bring their offerings—perhaps the Sabbath or end of a lunar season. We know that God established certain seasons for His people Israel to appear before Him, and they were not to come empty-handed. Likely it was with this understanding that we find these two brothers appearing before the Lord.

One interesting point is that Abel's offering was the first-born of his flock. There's good reason to believe that Abel received divine revelation of what later became known as the *tithe*. We read in Deuteronomy 12:5-6: *"But you shall seek the Lord at the place which the Lord your God shall choose from all your tribes, to establish His name there for His dwelling, and there you shall come. And there you shall bring your burnt offerings, your sacrifices, your tithes, the contribution of your hands, your votive offerings, your freewill offerings, and the first born of your herd and of your flock."*

Some argue that Abel's offering was accepted and Cain's rejected because Cain's was of the ground, and therefore without blood. However, Israel brought grain offerings to the Lord, which were accepted by Him—so we know this wasn't the case. We're told by the writer of Hebrews that God considered the person bringing the sacrifice as much, or more, than the he considered the sacrifice itself. In Hebrews Eleven, verse four, we read: *"By faith Abel offered to God a better sacrifice than Cain."* Apparently, Abel's faith played a major role in God's acceptance of his offering. How this faith was measured may well have been his attitude—God saw and delighted in the state of Abel's *heart*. We also read that Abel's sacrifice was *better;* this word can be translated as *greater* or *larger*. It seems that Abel brought an offering worthy of his God. Paul tells us: " . . . *the Lord loves a cheerful giver."* Perhaps Cain gave grudgingly and reluc-tantly while Abel gave cheerfully and bountifully. Man looks on the outward appearance, but God looks at the heart. The Psalmist understood this when, after grievously sinning with Bathsheba, he sought God's forgiveness and declared: *"For Thou dost not delight in sacrifice, otherwise I would give it. Thou art not pleased with burnt offering. The sacrifices of God are a broken spirit; a broken and a contrite heart, O God, Thou wilt not despise."* (Psalm 51:16, KJV) The writer of Hebrews also reminds us that God is *"able to judge the thoughts and intentions of the heart."* (Hebrews 4:12)

This may well have been the first tithe we read about in Scripture. Before Israel was established as a people or nation, Abraham paid tithes to Melchizedek. But many of the early church fathers believed that Cain and Abel's offerings were the beginning of tithing. Many of these early writers attributed the rejection of Cain's offering on the fact that he failed to bring the whole tithe to the Lord. Here is how A. Edwin Wilson makes this point: "Clement of Rome, in the first century, wrote that Cain's sin was in not bringing the first fruits as did Abel. Irenaeus, in the second century, wrote that the difference between Cain's and Abel's offerings was in fact that Abel brought a tithe of his flock, but Cain did not bring the tithes of his crops. Hilary, Bishop of Poictiers, in the fourth century, maintained that the experience of Cain and Abel told us that the command to tithe began in Eden. Hugo, Abbott of St Victor's, and Peter Comestor, in the twelfth century both maintained that God had respect unto Abel's offering because it was the tithe but had no respect unto Cain's because it was not the tithe. Grotius, in the seventh century, wrote that Cain did not offer the best, neither did he give the right proportion, the tenth, which from the ancient ages was the amount due to God." *(Selected Writings of A. Edwin Wilson. Arlen L. Chitwood, Editor. Published by Conley & Schoettle Publishing Co. Miami Springs, Fl 33166, page 300.)*

Whether or not these leaders were correct in their assessment of Cain and Abel's offerings as being the tithe, we can certainly learn from both of them. Do we withhold from God the sacrifices and offerings due His name, or do we willingly, lovingly, lavishly, and sacrificially bring the very best that we can bring Him? Keep in mind that the only acceptable sacrifice (from God's standpoint) was a *perfect* sacrifice. Every sacrifice was inspected by the priest—if any blemish was found, the sacrifice was rejected and declared unacceptable. Thankfully, we no longer have to bring an animal sacrifice to God—Jesus Himself is the perfect sacrifice. Paul reminds us in his letter to the Corinthians: *"He made Him who knew no sin to be sin on our behalf, so that we might become the righteousness of God in Him."* (2 Corinthians 5:21)

Although Jesus Christ has become our *sin offering,* we're reminded of other sacrifices that we can present to the Lord: The New Testament speaks of our bodies becoming a living sacrifice; we offer God a sacrifice of praise from the fruit of our lips, and our *giving* is considered a sacrifice. Just as the Old Testament priest inspected every sacrifice, I believe our Great High Priest—the Lord Jesus Christ—also inspects our sacrifices and offerings. When Jesus observed those who were giving at the Temple, He singled out a woman who gave only a small monetary gift. He declared that (in the eyes of the Lord) she'd given much more than anyone else. Likewise, we may have perfect pitch when we sing, but if our hearts are far from Him, our offerings are blemished. Like the Psalmist, our prayer should be: *"Let the words of my mouth and the meditation of my heart be acceptable in Thy sight." (Psalm 19:14)*

TWELVE

The First Sabbath

Although the Lord declared every day that He made as *good,* the seventh day was special; it was *blessed*: *"Then God blessed the seventh day and sanctified it, because in it He rested from all His work which God had created and made." (Genesis 2:3)* While the Sabbath marked the end of God's work, it was man's first day. God doesn't become weary or tired, and therefore He does not need to rest. We can assume then, as Jesus informed us, that the *Sabbath was made for man,* and not *man for the Sabbath.*

For over two thousand years men have debated the importance of the Sabbath. Did God intend a prescribed day, or a day for rest? If it was a prescribed day, then which day? The obvious answer to the Seventh-day Adventist is Saturday; but then, *which Saturday?* I've just been watching the opening of the American Embassy in Jerusalem and I noticed that there's an eight-hour difference between Arkansas time and the time in Israel. Our Sabbath days are almost a working day apart. Since most historians and expositors agree that Eden was located in the Middle East, we might assume that (to be biblically accurate) we should adjust our Sabbath to align with theirs. Perhaps you think I'm crazy, but my point is: which is more important — the day, or the purpose of the day?

Some fifty years ago, while ministering in Tonga, I learned an interesting fact. The Seventh-day Adventists there actually worship on Sunday, rather than Saturday because the International Date Line makes a jog around this little island nation. The Tongan government placed the date line east of Tonga for commercial reasons, so they'd have the same day as New Zealand and Fiji. Can you see how difficult it would be for anyone (other than those situated near Israel) to keep the original evening and morning of the Sabbath?

Let's face it: the Sabbath was made for *rest*. Arthur W. Pink writes: *"The next thing we would observe is that the Sabbath is not termed 'the seventh day of the week.' Nor is it ever so styled in Scripture! So far as the Old Testament is concerned, any day which was used for rest, and which was followed by six days of work, was a Sabbath! It's not correct, then, to say that the 'Sabbath' can only be observed on Saturday. There is not a word of Scripture to support such a statement."*

The fact that *rest* was more important than *the day* is shown in Exodus Twenty- Three, verse twelve: *"Six days you are to do your work, but on the seventh day you shall cease from labor in order that your ox and your donkey may rest, and the son of your female slave, as well as your stranger, may refresh themselves."* The point here is that long before He commanded Israel to keep a Sabbath of rest, God established this principle. My father used to say, "If you don't come apart and rest awhile, you'll come a part in a while."

THIRTEEN

The First Clean and Unclean Animals

Following the naming of the animals by Adam, God must have revealed to him that certain ones were considered *clean* and others *unclean*. We know that Noah was told by God to separate the animals (which he brought into the ark) by clean and unclean. For Noah to know which were clean and unclean, it must have been an established fact.

In looking through several commentaries on this matter there seems to be no agreement. However, if we assume that Moses wrote Genesis by Divine inspiration, surely he would have understood any difference between the Levitical laws regarding clean and unclean and the animals mentioned here. We're left with the understanding that the clean and unclean of Noah's day were no different than those given later by God to His people Israel.

In speaking of clean and unclean, we tend to assume the unclean were inferior, dirtier, or perhaps evil in some way. Yet we're told that after God created them, He saw that they *were good*—all of them. We're not told why God classified animals as clean and unclean. Perhaps it was to teach Israel the importance of *obedience* to God. Or, as one of my friends suggested, it was another way God chose to set Israel apart from the other nations. This truth seems to be borne out when God gave Moses the following instructions: *"You shall not eat anything which dies of itself. You may give it to the alien who is in your town, so that he may eat it, or you may sell it to a foreigner, for you are a holy people to the LORD your God." (Deuteronomy 14:21)* We know that God is no respecter of persons; so He was not trying to cause physical harm to the surrounding nations, but rather highlighting the fact that Israel was to be distinct from the world around them.

We do know that according to the New Covenant, the distinction between clean and unclean is no longer valid. Not only did Jesus declare all foods clean (Mark 7:19), but we read that this was no longer a requirement for the believer (according to the Jerusalem Council in Acts Chapter Fifteen). These things were all a part of the "seed truths" that later germinated in the daily lives of God's people, Israel.

FOURTEEN

The First Priesthood

We've already looked at the first priests back in Chapter Four. We explored the priestly role of Adam and Eve as they ministered to the Lord in daily fellowship while still in the garden. Now let's focus briefly on Melchizedek. We have no mention of him being in or around the garden at the time of Adam and Eve, but he played an important role in Abraham's life long before the establishment of the Levitical priesthood. Not only did Melchizedek precede the Levitical priesthood, he also supersedes it. We're told that Jesus is a priest *after the order of Melchizedek.*

Melchizedek is by far the most mysterious character in the Bible. He was King of Salem (an early name for Jerusalem) as well as priest of the Most High God. His name means "king of righteousness," and Salem means *peace*. What a beautiful picture of Jesus Christ, whose righteousness alone gives us peace. Melchizedek (being both king and priest) represents the "royal-priesthood" to which believers are all called. One Hebrew tradition suggests that Melchizedek was none other than Shem. But this tradition contradicts the scripture that says he was *"without father, without mother."* *(Hebrews 7:3)* There's also a widespread belief that he was the Lord Jesus Christ. This contradicts the fact that Melchizedek was *"made like the Son of God."* *(Hebrews 7:3)*

Herbert Lockyer, in his book *All the Kings and Queens of the Bible,* writes this of Melchizedek: "Melchizedek was both a king and priest. Under the Law there was an impassable barrier between royalty and priesthood, but because Melchizedek was a type of Christ he combined both offices and is presented as a king of righteousness and of peace, and as a priest of the Most High God. And the duties of the priesthood were not incompatible with the dignity of kinship. Taking no part in war with other kings, Melchizedek is a fitting type of Christ's peace-loving character.

"Priestly functions included the ministry of encouragement for the man who had fought God's battles. The bread and wine provided hospitable refreshment for the weary soldier and suggests another bringing forth of bread and wine (Luke 22:19), memorials of sacrifice. Then there was the bestowal of a benediction, "He blessed Abraham," and also the utterance of praise, "He blessed the most high God."...In his person, name, office, residence and government, Melchizedek is an eminent type of Christ. The death of the king of Salem is not recorded, which is suggestive of the endlessness of Christ's priesthood." *(Pages 188-189)*

This brief account of Melchizedek by Lockyer gives us sufficient insight into the fact that there existed a priesthood long before the Levitical priesthood. As I've already mentioned, I believe Adam and Eve were given the calling of functioning as both priests and kings. Some teach that we're either one or the other, but this is refuted by God's word when we are called a royal-priesthood.

Melchizedek will forever remain a mystery. Google his name and you will discover a plethora of opinions regarding him. Not until we arrive in heaven, our eternal home, will we know for sure who he is. Then we shall know even as we are known, for we will no longer see through a glass darkly, but face to face. What we do know now is that this Melchizedek priesthood existed prior to Israel's formation as a nation—and it'll continue long after the Aaronic priesthood has come and gone.

FIFTEEN

The First Law

The word *law* makes many people think of restrictions. Laws are considered negative. However, James speaks of the "law of liberty" and the "royal law." God's laws are not for our misery, but for our good.

The law of God expresses the mind of God and reveals His moral standard for regulating man's conduct. There is no list of Ten Commandments mentioned in Genesis, but God does tell Adam what to do and what not to do. The first command they received was: *"Be fruitful and multiply, and fill the earth, and subdue it . . ." (Genesis 1:28)* Society cannot function without certain rules and regulations. God is a God of order, and therefore He gave Adam and Eve the barest requirements possible to be both holy and happy. Consider this command that God gave to Adam: *"From any tree of the garden you may eat freely; but from the tree of the knowledge of good and evil you shall not eat, for in the day you eat from it you shall surely die."* (Genesis 2:16-17) Before God told them *what not to eat,* He said they could freely eat from *any* of the other trees. Only one tree carried the death penalty. Never consider God mean-spirited because of this command; God must be praised for thinking of their happiness and well being. God's laws should not be viewed as restrictions, but as blessings.

Without consequences, laws appear as mere suggestions. God had no choice; He had to drive man out of the garden after their disobedience. Likewise, Cain was punished for killing his brother Abel. What's so remarkable about God's law is that it can all be fulfilled by the two greatest commandments: "Love the Lord Thy God" and "Love your neighbor as yourself." The following short article explains how one command is connected to another; long before we read of the Ten Commandments we see them implied by man's first sin:

"The One True God has had a standard of righteous conduct that began at the time of the Creation of Adam and Eve and hasn't changed since. Just by looking at the first sin committed by Adam and Eve we can see that they have transgressed against many of the Ten Commandments. Whoever or whatever someone obeys and serves is his god. In this case, Adam and Eve, by obeying the serpent broke the First Commandment. They had *"put another god before the One True God."* In doing so, they also broke the Fifth Commandment by *"dishonoring their Parent,"* in the sense that Adam was a created *son* of God (Luke 3:38). Their sin also involved *"stealing"* (the Eighth Commandment), in that they took the forbidden fruit that wasn't theirs. Putting the blame on someone else instead of taking responsibility for one's own sin is breaking the Ninth Commandment of *"bearing false witness against one's neighbor." (Gen. 3:12-13)* Besides this, Eve *"lusted"* for the forbidden fruit. Lusting is coveting, which breaks the Tenth Commandment.

"Breaking one commandment leads to breaking all of them. This is precisely what the apostle James expressed in James 2:10: *"For whoever shall keep the whole law, and yet stumble in one point, he is guilty of all."* God's laws are interrelated and intricately woven together — if you break one, you eventually break them all.

"Learning from the mistakes of Adam and Eve we today must be thankful and content to be living by His word. The key to finding true happiness is in obeying God's commandments and doing His will." *(God's First Commandment to Mankind, by Arkwriter, Monday, 22 June 2009.)*

SIXTEEN

The First Prophet

Over the last sixteen chapters we've explored the Gentile roots (or seeds) that ultimately blossomed into Israel's way of life and spiritual service to God. Now let's look at some of the spiritual fathers who preceded Jacob or Israel.

I've always enjoyed Bible characters; they're real people, and not fabricated superstars or aliens that I cannot relate to. The first character we will look at is Enoch — one of the most interesting men in the Bible. He was one of only two men who never died a natural death but was taken into heaven while still alive. All who lived prior to Enoch died. But of Enoch we're told: *"And he was not, for God took him."* (*Genesis 5:24*) We don't have many details about his life, but we can piece together his exceptional qualities by comparing what we know of him with scriptural truths.

The writer of Hebrews says of Enoch: *"He had this testimony, that he was pleasing to God." (Hebrews 11:5 KJV)* We read in the book of Revelation: *" . . . for Thou didst create all things, and for Thy pleasure they were created." (Revelation 4:11 KJV)* Little wonder then that Enoch was pleasing to God—he fulfilled his God given destiny or purpose. The Father said the very same thing of Jesus: *"This is my beloved Son in whom I am well pleased." (Matthew 3:17)* We tend to think God loves us because of our actions—but we don't read of any accomplishments that made Enoch admirable. It appears that it wasn't so much what Enoch did as *who Enoch was.* We live in a time when success is measured more by achievement than by attitude; more by performance than piety. But God is much more concerned with *character* than with conquest.

Lest there be any confusion, this is not the same Enoch that was a son of Cain. We're told that this Enoch was the seventh from Adam. By the time Enoch lived, the wickedness of man had steadily increased to the point where men were consumed with evil *continually.* This was the culture and environment where Enoch lived—and he pleased God. Men often make excuses for their behavior by blaming culture, surroundings or parentage. Enoch's life testifies that we're all without excuse in this regard.

In Genesis we read that it was *after* Enoch became the father of Methuselah that he *"walked with God."* (*Genesis 5:22*) He was sixty-five years old when he became a father. Alexander White, in his book on Bible characters, suggests this was a pivotal point in Enoch's life — this new responsibility could have been the motivating factor for change. Perhaps he suddenly realized that there were two little eyes and ears observing and listening to him — he was now a role model for good or evil; he was a letter *"known and read by all men."* (*2 Corinthians 3:2*) Sometimes it takes a major event or crisis to get our attention and turn our lives around — the birth of Methuselah may have had this impact on Enoch.

What we do know is that Enoch chose to live for God, despite the wickedness of those around him. In the Old Testament we read an interesting phrase (repeatedly): *" . . . he did . . . according to all that his father David had done."* We need more men and women who inspire us to live lives of godliness, rather than allowing Hollywood or the world to set the example for our children and us. Paul rebuked the Jews, telling them: *"The name of God is blasphemed among the Gentile because of you."* (*Romans 2:24*)

One of the first poems I memorized after becoming a Christian was, "I'd Rather See a Sermon," by Edgar A. Guest. It's still one of my all time favorites:

I'd rather see a sermon
Than hear one any day.
I'd rather one would walk with me
Than merely tell the way.

The eye's a better pupil
And more willing than the ear,
Fine counsel is confusing
But example's always clear.

And the best of all the preachers
Are the men who live their creeds.
For to see good put in action
Is what everybody needs.

I soon can learn to do it
If you'll let me see it done
I can watch your hands in action,
But your tongue too fast may run.

And the lectures you deliver
May be very wise and true.
But I'd rather get my lessons
By observing what you do;

For I might misunderstand you
And the high advice you give.
But there's no misunderstanding
How you act and how you live.

The First Prophet

We often fail to realize the influence our lives have on those around us. What a person *says* is eclipsed by what he *does*. When we're told *"Enoch walked with God,"* the term "walked" (in the Bible) describes much more than our stride. It speaks of actions or behavior. The prophet Amos reminds us: *" . . . two cannot walk together unless they be agreed."* *(Amos 3:3)* This biblical principle tells us volumes about Enoch. Other scriptures tell us that "bad company corrupts good morals," so we can assume that the more Enoch walked with God, the more he took on God's character or likeness. Enoch grew in his relationship and knowledge of God — as you spend time with an individual, you gain more knowledge and understanding of them.

When Jesus descended from a night of prayer, before appointing and commissioning the twelve disciples, we're told: *"He appointed twelve that they might be with Him . . ."* *(Mark 4:14)* The first priority of the twelve wasn't preaching or casting out demons, but being with the Lord. Much later, John wrote: *"What was from the beginning, what we have heard, what we have seen with our eyes, what we beheld and our hands have handled, concerning the Word of Life . . ."* *(1 John 1:1)* John was an effective communicator of what Jesus was like — he'd seen Him, touched Him and heard Him. Imagine how difficult it would be to describe someone you had never met. Enoch then, like John, must have known God in a way that few others would know Him.

91

Walking, from a physical point of view, implies a slow and steady pace—as opposed to a sudden burst of speed that can't be maintained. Hundreds of years after Enoch, God spoke to Abraham and said: " . . . *walk before me and be blameless." (Genesis 17:1)* The implication is that God let Abraham know that he was being observed. But of Enoch we're told: *"He walked with God."* I'm reminded of what the prophet Micah wrote: *"He has shown you, O man, what is good and what does the Lord require of Thee, but to do justly, love mercy and to walk humbly with thy God." (Micah 6:8)* All of these qualities must have been in Enoch's life if he walked with God and was found pleasing to Him. Perhaps it was Enoch who inspired Paul to exhort the believers in Thessalonica with these words: *"We request and exhort you . . . as to how you ought to walk and please God." (1 Thessalonians 4:1)*

We admire men who lived long, godly lives. Yet no one comes close Enoch—we're not told of any time during his three hundred years when he doubted God or became discouraged.

The term *pleased God* speaks of something higher than just being loved by God. Too many people rely on the fact that God loves them, yet they fail to understand that they may not be pleasing to Him. The prophet Malachi declared to the children of Israel that God loved them, but then several verses later God stated: *"I am not pleased with you." (Malachi 1:10)* As the father of three daughters,

I have never ceased to love them; however, there were times when they failed to please me. Bringing pleasure to God is the highest and greatest act possible. Jesus said, *"For I always do the things that are pleasing to Him." (John 8:29)* The Apostle Paul stated, *"We have as our ambition, whether at home or absent to be pleasing to Him." (2 Corinthians 5:9)* These verses help us to understand what type of a person Enoch was and the testimony he had before God.

I've often asked myself, *How did Enoch please God?* We're told in the book of Hebrews: *"Now faith is the assurance of things hoped for and the conviction of things not seen. For by it the men of old gained approval . . . and without faith it's impossible to please Him . . ." (Hebrews 11:1-2,6)* Reading about Enoch, we tend to think of him *seeing* God with his natural eyes. But if that were the case, there would be no need for faith. It was his faith that brought pleasure to God. We often walk by feelings instead of faith—but Enoch's faith was unwavering. How do we know? The writer of Hebrews tells us: *" . . . but My righteous one shall live by faith, and if he shrinks back, My soul has no pleasure in him." (Hebrews 10:38)* Enoch had the testimony of pleasing God, so he must have been steadfast in his faith.

Another truth we see is that Enoch was *dead* to the desires of the flesh. I say this because of Paul's word to the Romans: *"They that are in the flesh cannot please God." (Romans 8:8)* Enoch desired God's presence; he wasn't motivated by his flesh, but by his spirit. Enoch appears to have lived a sanctified or separated life. Paul reminds Timothy: *"No soldier in active service entangles himself in the affairs of everyday life, so that he may please the one who enlisted him as a soldier."* *(2 Timothy 2:4)* These scriptures all refer to *pleasing* the Lord. It would be impossible to have a testimony of pleasing the Lord if Enoch violated these principles.

Another value that set this man apart from his generation was the fact that he walked in moral purity. Paul reminds us of the importance of this in his letter to the believers in Thessalonica. Here is what he wrote: *" . . . we request and exhort you in the Lord Jesus, that, as you received from us instruction as to how you ought to walk and please God . . . For this is the will of God, your sanctification; that you abstain from sexual immorality . . ."* *(1 Thessalonians 4:1-3)* Keep in mind that Enoch lived in a time when the thoughts of every man's heart were *only evil continually.*

Another great attribute of Enoch's life was his fear of God. We know that in order to walk with God consistently for three hundred years Enoch must have hated what his God hated and loved what his God loved. The Psalmist tells us: *"The Lord takes pleasure in them that fear Him."* *(Psalm 147:11)* With this verse in mind, we can conclude that one reason Enoch had the testimony he did was that he feared God. One more secret to Enoch's life was that he walked in daily obedience to the voice of God. John tells us to: *"Do the things that are pleasing* in His sight." (1 John 3:22) Since there was no *written word* in those days, Enoch must have learned to hear God's voice—as well as his own conscience. He responded to these gentle urgings with obedience, thereby bringing God pleasure.

As for me, I don't want a false sense of peace in the knowledge that God loves me—for that isn't *my* testimony but it's His. I want to have the same testimony that Enoch had, that of being pleasing to the Lord.

We must look at one final thing about Enoch: Jude tells us that Enoch *prophesied.* This is the first mention in the Bible of anyone prophesying, and it opens up a new realm of insight into this great man's life. It reveals that he was a deeply spiritual man who understood the moving of the Holy Spirit and who must have sought God concerning things to come. Perhaps he carried a burden for those around him and paved the way for God's deliverance and judgment in Noah's day. What we know for sure is that God gave Enoch a revelation of the return of the Lord in judgment on the ungodly. Let's read what Jude wrote: *"And about these also, Enoch, in the seventh generation from Adam, prophesied, saying, 'Behold the Lord came with many thousands of His holy ones, to execute judgment upon all, and to convict all the ungodly of all their ungodly deeds which they had done in an ungodly way, and of all the harsh things which ungodly sinners have spoken against Him.'"* (Jude 14-15)

Don't be confused by Enoch's use of the phrase "the Lord came," as though he was referring to the past rather than the present. Prophets often spoke of things to come as though they were already past. They did this for two reasons: to show the certainty, and to show the nearness of Christ's coming.

Lastly, we're told of Enoch's unusual departure from this earth, which was unlike all others except for Elijah. The Rev. James Jenkyn, M A. describes Enoch's departure in his exposition of The Epistle Of Jude, written in 1652 (page 301): "This prophet was famous both for his piety and privileges; he was not only eminent for his piety in walking with God, which was his own benefit, and for his public usefulness in warning and instructing that corrupt age in which he lived, keeping up the name of God in the world, opposing the profaneness of his times; but also for that glorious and unheard of privilege of being taken to God, who thereby proclaimed him to be fit for no company but his own, and one for whom no place was good enough but heaven; a child, yet sent abroad into the world as the rest, yet whom his Father so tenderly loved, that he wouldn't suffer him to stay half so long from home as his other children; one who had done much work in a little time, and who having made a proficiency in that heavenly art of holiness above all his fellows, had that high degree of heavenly glory conferred upon him long before the ordinary time."

Dr. B. H. Carrolls, in his expository work of Genesis, says this about Enoch's transition to glory: "God translated him. This is an old Latin word, an irregular verb, and it usually means carried over or carried across. God carried him across. Across what? Across death. Death is the river that divides this world from the world to come, and here was a man that never did go through that river at all. When he got there God carried him across. God transferred him; translated him; God picked him up and carried him over and put him on the other shore. And walking along here in time and communing with God by faith, in an instant he was communing with God by sight in another world. Faith, O precious faith! Faith had turned to sight, and hope had turned to fruition in a single moment. The life of faith was thus crowned by entrance into the life of perfect fellowship above, *'And they shall walk with Me in white.' (Rev. 3:4)*"

The scripture sums up his life far more succinctly by declaring: *"And he was not found, for God took him up." (Hebrews 11:5)*

SEVENTEEN

The First Mention of Grace

Everyone, from the age of three to one hundred and three, seems to know the story of Noah. He is one of the best-known characters in the Bible—not so much for who he was, but for what he did. Because of what he constructed, we often forget about his character.

Noah was the great grandson of Methuselah and the grandson of Enoch. His father Lamech seemed to have an understanding that God had cursed the ground he toiled on. Noah traces his heritage back to three generations of God-fearing men.

We're told that Noah lived in a time of unprecedented evil—Jesus described it as similar to the days in which we now live. Man was consumed by every conceivable evil. It began in the mind and eventually found its expression through the body. This grieved Almighty God so much that He regretted creating man. This alone reveals how utterly depraved man had become and how sin grieves the heart of God. Not only was God grieved by what He saw and heard, but He took the ultimate step of saying that He would destroy man from the face of the earth – the same earth He previously declared to be *very good*.

However, after God's decision to destroy man, we read these words of hope: *"But Noah found grace in the eyes of the Lord."* (Genesis 6:8) God saw two things: he saw the wickedness of man, but he also saw Noah. What was it about Noah that caused Him to reconsider? In Genesis 7:1 we read: *"Enter the ark, you and your household; for you alone I have seen to be righteous before Me in this time."* According to the book of Hebrews, Noah *"walked with God."* Like Enoch, he walked righteously before God in the midst of a crooked and perverse generation. These men remind us that we cannot blame our lack of godliness on the conditions around us – and our choices have tremendous consequences. Consider what we read in Psalm 106:23: after the children of Israel forsook God and worshipped the golden calf, God determined to destroy the entire nation. But then we read theses words: *"Had not Moses, His chosen one, stood in the breach before Him, to turn away His wrath from destroying them . . ."* Often in the Bible we see one man making all the difference.

Noah found *grace*. This is the first time grace is mentioned in God's word. Notice that it wasn't until sin was manifest that grace was also manifest. Noah *found* grace; he didn't earn it or exchange something for it. Grace was not a product of his own making or discipline but rather something he found. Since this is the first mention of *grace*, it's important to see the exact context it which it appears—it's used in contrast to an evil and adulterous generation marked by rebellion, greed and lust. Grace, then, is God's empowering to live free from the power of sin.

Grace never condones sin in any way, shape, or form. Grace is not a weakness in God's character that causes Him to overlook or wink at sin, as if to say, "It's okay once in a while, I understand." Never! Here is how G. Campbell Morgan describes it: "When a man turns the grace of God into lasciviousness, when he consents to act upon the idea that because he stands in grace, and therefore his conduct is of very little moment, he is apostatizing. That is the most terrible of all apostasies. There have been periods when that apostasy has been formulated into a definite doctrine; the antinomian heresy declared that because a man is in Christ he cannot be lost, and therefore it matters little what his conduct may be, because nothing he can do can sever as between Christ and himself. That is apostasy in its worst form. No man can hold that doctrine without denying the Lord and Master.

That is to deny everything for which He stood; to deny the real meaning and purpose of His dying, to deny the whole purpose of His heart, as He came to destroy the works of the devil, in order to make possible to man a life of purity, to save man not merely from the punishment of sin, but from sin itself. To continue in sin that grace may abound is to deny the perfection of His Person; the passion of His heart that bore Him through the Cross; and His purpose for the establishment of the Kingdom of God in righteousness and holiness through the whole world." *(Living Messages of the Books of the Bible; Fleming H. Revel; page 199)*

It was this God-given grace that caused Noah to stand head and shoulders above his fellow man and live a life of justice and righteousness. Charles Spurgeon reminds us: *"'Noah was a gracious man,'* one in whom the Lord had shown great favor, for he had put grace in his heart, and had given him faith, for it was by faith that Noah *'prepared an ark to the saving of his house; by which he condemned the world, and became heir of the righteousness which is by faith.'* The grace of God was within him, and became the source and wellspring from which flowed the righteousness for which he was so remarkable. Grace is the root of every righteous character, so let grace have the honor and glory of it."

We're also told that Noah was a just man and perfect in his generation. These two qualities are both *attributes of God Almighty.* God is just and righteous in all his ways, as well as exhorting us to be perfect as our heavenly Father is perfect. Spurgeon goes on to say: "We're told that *'Noah was a just man.'* It's especially noticeable that, in an age of violence and oppression, Noah was a just man. He was no oppressor; he dealt justly and fairly with his fellow men. Noah was also "perfect in his generations"; the marginal reading is that he was "upright". He wasn't one who leaned this way for advantage, or who leaned this way for gain; he stood upright in conscious integrity before his fellows. Acting in accordance with the grace of God which was in his heart, he learned to do that which was just towards others." Like his ancestor Enoch, he lived in communion with God, in prayerfulness and pious meditation, and his life before his fellow men was in consistency with that walk before God.

In his letter to the Corinthians, Paul reminds us: " . . . *whatever was written in earlier times was for our instruction, that through the perseverance and encouragement of the Scriptures we might have hope."* *(1 Corinthians 15:4)* As we look into God's word, we must keep in mind that these are not *idle words* that God told Moses, but *"indeed it is your life."* *(Deuteronomy 32:47)* God the Holy Spirit saw to it that the lives of these men were recorded here for our instruction, that we too might be *"trained in righteousness."* *(2 Timothy 3:16)* We tend to place men like Enoch and Noah on a pedestal, as though they were the exception to the rule. When comparing our lives to theirs, we make every imaginable excuse for why we cannot attain to their stature. But this was never in the mind of the Spirit when inspiring their stories to be written. They are recorded to show us that we too—through the grace of God—can attain to that same standard. We must remember that as we study the lives of these men.

When we speak of Noah's righteousness, we're not implying *perfection*. Noah had flaws. But God saw his that heart was to live in a manner pleasing to the Lord; refusing to be conformed to this world, he sought to be transformed by the Spirit of God. And as for Noah's faith, it was rooted in the nature and character of God. He believed in God and trusted His word—in this case, God's spoken word that He planned to destroy the earth with a flood. Noah's faith was active; faith without works is dead, but Noah put his faith to work and built an ark, in response to God's word.

The fulfillment of God's word to Noah didn't come to pass for a hundred years. This tells us something of the trying of Noah's faith and also the steadfastness of his faith. It's always easy to look back on the accomplishments of faith and rejoice in what God did. It's another thing to endure the months and years of believing for something without doubting or allowing discouragement to cripple our faith. We're told Noah built an ark with a specific purpose in mind, a goal to achieve: he built an ark for the salvation of his family.

Noah's family is never mentioned as being *righteous,* and yet we're not told that Noah built an ark for *himself,* but for *his house.* Too often, when we read of Noah, we imagine a vast assembling of animals crowded into the ark. While that is true, the main purpose of the ark was not to save the *pets,* but to save Noah and his family.

Jesus reminded His disciples (in Matthew, when He spoke concerning the signs of the last days): *"For the coming of the Son of Man will be just like the days of Noah. For as in those days which were before the flood they were eating and drinking, they were marrying and giving in marriage until the day that Noah entered the ark, and they did not understand until the flood came and took them all away; so shall the coming of the Son of Man be." (Matthew 24:37-39)* These verses serve as a warning to every man of God that he too should be preparing an ark for the salvation of his family; a flood is coming that will sweep away all who are unprepared for the Lord's return. As parents we must take these "days" seriously, encouraging our children to avail themselves of God's amazing grace in their lives.

Noah believed God's warning of impending destruction. Do we take His warnings seriously, or are we like those who sneer and ask, *"Where is the promise of His coming?" (2 Peter 3:4)* Noah was a *"preacher of righteousness." (2 Peter 2:5)* This statement reveals another of Noah's outstanding qualities: he had compassion for souls. Noah was concerned about his needs, and those of his family, but he also concerned himself with the needs of those around him. It's easy to settle into a state of complacency after making Christ the Lord of our lives, while forgetting the multitudes that are still perishing. Once again, I'm staggered by Noah's faithfulness; he continued preaching year after year (for over a hundred years) without any known results! Another fact we learn from Noah's life was that while he feared God (reverential fear), he had no fear of man. The word "preacher" means one who proclaims or heralds a message. Noah stood alone against a generation of men and women who had little or no interest in what he proclaimed, and yet we never read of him quitting or slowing down. What a man!

One last statement we read about Noah is that " . . . *he condemned the world." (Hebrews 11:7)* This doesn't infer that Noah went about speaking words of condemnation, gleefully waiting for their destruction. No, nothing like that; but he was rather like his Master, weeping over their lost condition. I'll never forget when Pastor Tommy Faulk, a preacher friend of mine, told me of a vision he had of God's judgment on the lost. As each person was brought before the Lord to be judged, the Lord bowed His head and could barely look at the person as He began sobbing uncontrollably; He then pointed in the direction of Hell, and they were led away. This should be the attitude of all believers toward the lost, rather than delighting in their eternal fate. The Bible tells us this about God through the prophet Ezekiel: *"'Do I have any pleasure in the death of the wicked,' declares the Lord GOD, 'rather than that he should turn from his ways and live?'"* (*Ezekiel 18:23*)

Forty years ago, two of our three daughters attended the Agape Force School in East Texas. In those days the Agape Force were producing songs for children with the sole purpose of teaching them godly conduct and character formation. Some genuinely gifted young men and women were involved in their media department. On one of their vinyl recordings they had composed a song about Noah and the flood. In order to teach the children about God's displeasure at the sinful condition of the world, and why he had to destroy it, they described God as crying for forty days and forty nights. His tears flooded the earth with water. We know that wasn't the case, nevertheless, it conveys God's pain (rather than pleasure) at destroying the world.

We read in Peter's epistle that after Jesus' death in the flesh he descended into Hades, *" . . . and made proclamation to the spirits now in prison, who once were disobedient, when the patience of God kept waiting in the days of Noah, during the construction of the ark, in which a few, that is, eight persons, were brought safely through the water."* (*1 Peter 3:19-20*) Noah was 500 years old when he began to build the ark and 600 years old when he entered it. We're not told whether or not he spent all that time constructing the ark. However, we do know: " . . . *the patience of God kept waiting." (1 Peter 3:20)* If God already knew who was going to enter the ark, why did he wait?

God patience! What a beautiful thought—God is prepared to wait for change to take place in our lives. But I often remind those I minister to that we shouldn't confuse *God's patience* with *God's permission.* When God doesn't immediately judge us in some way for our actions, we might misinterpret His patience for His permission to continue. We're told in the book of Revelation (concerning the woman Jezebel) that God said, *"And I gave her time to repent." (Revelation 2:21)* God certainly did not condone her actions, but He waited patiently, hoping she would repent. Only in eternity will we look back and truly understand just how patient God was with us.

EIGHTEEN

The First Spiritual Father

We're told that Abraham was the "father" of all who believe. For those who never had a spiritual father, now you do! As I've stated many times, fathers can have a profound impact on our lives—for good or evil. If your father was a mechanic, chances are you enjoy tinkering with cars. If your father was a lawyer, no doubt you're familiar with legalese. If your father enjoyed spaghetti, chances are you do too. Those may be some of the less important side effects of a father's influence. But what if your father was a racist? You might have struggled to understand or accept racial equality.

Fathers impact us; Abraham is no exception. As our spiritual father he is our role model, guide, or tutor. Much of what Abraham experienced in his walk of faith is similar to what each of us will experience. Abraham was a Gentile who became known as a Hebrew. *"Then the fugitive came and told Abram the Hebrew . . ." (Genesis 14:13)* We could also say he was the first disciple; God asked him to leave his father, mother, brothers and sisters and follow Him in obedience. While the wording is not exactly the same, the challenge to *forsake all* was identical.

The very first detail we're told about Abraham doesn't come from the Old Testament, but from the New. We read in the book of Acts: *"The God of glory appeared unto our father Abraham when he was in Mesopotamia, before he lived in Haran." (Acts 7:2)* I believe this was the definitive turning point in Abraham's life. (He wasn't known by the name Abraham initially, but by Abram.) As you begin studying Abraham's life (beginning in Genesis Chapter Twelve) you immediately see his radical obedience to God when he's commanded to leave his home and family. In the book of Acts, Stephen reveals (by inspiration of the Holy Spirit) that what preceded Abraham's obedience was an encounter with *"the God of glory."* This pattern appears in the Scriptures again and again; REVELATION PRECEDES CONSECRATION.

Paul, on the Damascus road, first had a revelation of God's blinding Shekinah brightness; afterwards he cried out, *"Lord what will you have me to do?"* Paul's *consecration* was preceded by *revelation.* Another example is the prophet Isaiah who, upon entering the Temple, had a revelation of the awesome holiness of God, whereupon he cried out, *"Here am I. Send me!"* Moses also first experienced a bush that was never consumed by the fire. Following this revelation, Moses quickly responded to God's call to return to the very land he had fled from forty years earlier. Even Ruth saw something in Naomi that caused her to leave her mother and father, along with their gods, and follow Naomi to a land and people different from her own. And Nathanael, who was initially skeptical of any good thing coming out of Nazareth, immediately changed his mind when Jesus revealed that he had seen him under the fig tree. That revelation changed this doubter to a believer. Over and over we see this principle operating. It would be safe to say that unless a person has experienced some revelation of God's glory, then chances are there's little true consecration. This occurs before marriage. A man begins to develop a relationship with a woman and as that relationship grows he becomes more and more aware of how wonderful she is. It isn't long before he makes a commitment to marriage. First came *revelation,* then *consecration.*

Returning then to Abraham: Following his encounter with the God of glory, we see his willingness to leave everything. How exactly God appeared and revealed His glory we're not told, but suffice to say Abraham's response was obedience. These first few verses of Genesis Twelve are packed with spiritual truth. God's first requirement of Abraham was one of *separation*. God can never use a person unless they are prepared to leave behind their former way of life, take up their cross and follow Him. This is the first requirement for all true disciples. I like to think of Abraham as the first disciple in the Bible. God asked him to forsake father, mother, brother and sister and follow Him.

God required of Abraham three areas of separation. The first was to leave his country or nation. God never asks us to give up or forsake something without replacing it with something better. For example: One day Jesus asked to borrow a fisherman's boat; He returned it full of fish. On another occasion He borrowed a little boy's lunch to feed the multitude. One preacher suggested that at the end of the day Jesus sent His disciples back to the boy's house with twelve baskets of leftovers. We know Jesus said, *"Truly I say to you, there is no one who has left house or brothers or sisters or mother or father or children or farms, for My sake and for the gospel's sake, but that he will receive a hundred times as much now in the present age, houses and brothers and sisters and mothers and children and farms, along with persecutions; and in the age to come, eternal life." (Mark 10:29-30)* This verse clearly reveals that when we give something to the Lord there's always more received than first given. Abraham was no exception. God asked him to give up his country or nation, but He made him the father of his own nation—Israel. He asked him to give up his relatives, but He promised him, in exchange, that his seed would bless the world. Last, and possibly most important, Abraham was asked to leave *his father's house*. I'm convinced that, at this time, Abraham didn't really grasp the magnitude of God's purpose behind these words. "His father's house" represents both Abraham's security and his identity. God was going to make Abraham a father of many nations; therefore, he had to leave his earthly father. God would be his provision and security; he had to leave behind the security of his father's house. As for his identity, God promised to make Abraham's name *great*. I'm going to leave the remaining promise, of blessing the nations, for another chapter where I can deal with it more fully.

Following these promises of blessing, we find Abraham building an altar, pitching his tent and digging a well. The altar, tent and well are mentioned frequently throughout Abraham's life. Allow me to expound a little on these three symbols: The ALTAR speaks of CONSECRATION and deals with our attitude toward SELF. The Altar was the place of sacrifice, surrender and death. The Altar always demanded the best. Nothing worthless, defiled or blemished would ever be accepted by God. The Altar required all, everything, the whole and not just a portion. The Altar reminds us to ask, "Am I prepared to offer God the very best, my all?"

The TENT speaks of PROGRESSION or CHANGE. After Abraham left his father's house we never read of him ever living in a house again. The writer of Hebrews tells us: *"By faith he lived as an alien in the land of promise, as in a foreign land, dwelling in tents with Isaac and Jacob . . ."* (Hebrews 11:9) TENTS are TRANSPORTABLE and easily moved. Unlike a house, that becomes an anchor and keeps you returning to it, a tent allows you to travel. The Psalmist wrote prophetically about the Bride when he wrote these words in Psalm Forty Five: *"Forget your people and your father's house; then the King will desire your beauty . . . she will be led to the King in embroidered work; the virgins, her companions who follow her, will be brought to Thee. They will be led forth with gladness and rejoicing; they will enter into the King's palace."* (Psalm 45:10-11,14-15) No groom desires his bride to remain in her father's house. She must be willing to forsake all others, lose her security and identity and come under a new authority. While it may be popular these days to leave the word *obey* out of wedding vows, that won't work with God! God requires obedience in everything, but the return gained is always worth more than the sacrifice. We've all used the phrase "in our house," meaning we lived by certain rules etc. A house represents authority and lifestyle. In the New Testament, the old wineskin (that has lost its flexibility or adaptability) represents this concept. There are tens of thousands of professing-believers who are unwilling to leave their "father's house." They refuse to allow God to have His way and insist

on functioning the way their family or denomina-
tion functioned fifty or a hundred years ago.

The third symbol is the WELL, which speaks
of SATISFACTION. This is the place we derive our
life from. Israel was severely reprimanded by God
through the prophet Jeremiah when he wrote: *"My
people have committed two evils: They have forsaken
Me, the fountain of living waters, to hew out for themselves cisterns, broken cisterns that can hold no water."*
(Jeremiah 2:13) He goes on to explain: *"What are you
doing on the road to Egypt, to drink the waters of the
Nile? Or what are you doing on the road to Assyria to
drink the waters of the Euphrates?" (Jeremiah 2:13,18)*

These three symbols then became the key to
Abraham's life. He was prepared to give God
everything. He was prepared to follow God wherever he was told to go. And he derived his life from
God. No wonder then he is referred to three times
as God's friend! However, we shouldn't place him
on a pedestal; Abraham was a man no different than
you and I. He made some major mistakes — notably
that of going to Egypt during a time of famine. There
Abraham sought to pawn off his wife as his sister, in
order to save his own skin. There he acquired Hagar,
whose lineage became Israel's greatest enemy.

Volumes could be (and have been) written
about Abraham. I don't intend to discuss every
nook and cranny of his life, but I want to look at
Chapter Fifteen of Genesis together. Here we find
God visiting Abraham and telling him not to fear.

Abraham had just fought against several kings in order to rescue his nephew Lot. No doubt Abraham began to fear for his life, thinking they might retaliate. God assured him, *"Do not fear Abram, I am a shield to you; your reward will be very great." (Genesis 15:1)* Abraham then asked God what God would give him, since he had no children. It appears that Abraham was contemplating his future, wondering if he'd end up turning over everything to his servant Eliezer. We then read: *"Since Thou hast given no offspring to me, one born in my house is my heir." (Genesis 12:2)* This was not Abraham's finest moment; he was accusing God of failing to give him any offspring. But God responded by taking Abraham outside and telling him to look up at the heavens and count the stars, adding *"So shall your descendants be." (Verse 5)* Just as God gave Noah the *rainbow* as a sign of His promise to never destroy the World with another flood, here God gave Abraham the *stars* as a guarantee of how many children would come from his loins. Any time Abraham doubted God's promise, all he had to do was look at the stars.

Not only did God promise to give Abraham posterity, but also possession of the land on which he trod. But again, Abraham's reaction was one of doubt. *"O Lord God, how may I know that I shall possess it?" (Verse 8)* We often react in the same way; we receive a word from the Lord and then immediately begin to doubt it will ever happen. There are some key points here: First comes *The Promise*, then *The Perplexity*, and lastly, *The Price*; every promise comes with a price tag. God responds to Abraham's question by telling him the cost: *"Bring Me a three year old heifer, and a three year old female goat, and a three year old ram, and a turtledove, and a young pigeon." (Verse 9)*

The promises of God don't simply fall into our laps without us paying some price. Take Joseph, who—after being bullied by his jealous brothers—was given an amazing *promise*. He had a dream in which he saw his brothers all bowing down before him. I'm convinced he hurried to breakfast the next morning fully expecting his dream to be fulfilled. After all, in the dream he saw his brothers just as they were when he went to bed that evening. He didn't see them as they would look some thirteen years later. The *price* Joseph had to pay to see the fulfillment of his dream was costly indeed; his brothers tried to kill him, and God tried him.

Returning to Abraham, we see him bringing together the sacrifices God required. We don't read of him building an altar on this occasion, but he must have done so. These verses can be read in a matter of seconds, and yet hours and hours of labor were involved. Not only did he select the finest animals, but they had to be killed and then divided in two. Finally they were placed on the altar—which first had to be erected. After having paid the price, I'm sure Abraham fully expected God to keep His promise by either answering by fire or speaking to him in some way. But after the price was paid, *The Predators* arrived; birds of prey swept down, seeking to steal or devour the very sacrifices Abraham had just presented to God.

The lesson here is obvious. The birds of prey represent the enemy — who does his best to thwart our attempts to carry out the will of God. I've often said, "Once you make a sacrificial commitment to the Lord, all hell will break loose." The enemy hates any sacrifice; he'll do all that's in his power to stop us from making them. However, Abraham refused to give ground to the enemy; he resisted the enemy's attempts to rob God of his offering. It wasn't a quick rebuke, but a steady, consistent driving away of the attacks as they swept around his sacrifices. The attack continued all day, with no sign of God's intervention. Do you ever feel that God has left you alone in the midst of some devilish attack? If so, you know how Abraham felt. He kept his side of the agreement, but God didn't appear. To make things worse, the sun began to set; darkness was enveloping Abraham. *"Terror and great darkness fell upon him." (Verse 12)* During this low point — which the old mystics referred to as *the dark night of the soul* — God told Abraham details which He withheld during His initial promise. Abraham now learned that his promised progeny would face tremendous pressure and persecution. Like Joseph before him, Abraham hadn't been given all of the details at first. Joseph saw himself being vindicated — not rejected further by his brothers. He didn't expect separation, accusation, and incarceration before his final exoneration, promotion and exaltation. Now Abraham learns that his descendants will be enslaved and oppressed for four hundred years before being liberated. God seldom shares everything He has in store for us all at once but rather gradually, as we need to know.

The darkness around Abraham reached the point where we read it was *"very dark."* The sun had set and a new day began. During the night we usually see the stars and moon, which God created to give light, but on this night it was *very dark*. When it's very dark, the stars (signs of God's faithfulness to His promises) cannot be seen. But someone once said, "Never doubt in the dark what God has shown you in the light." Abraham now had to walk by faith, and not by sight. We read: *" . . . on that day the Lord made a covenant with Abraham." (Verse 18)* In the New Testament Abraham is referred to as *"the father of all who believe."* Therefore, you should expect to see God deal with you in a similar fashion — and keep in mind that it's *"to do good for you in the end." (Deuteronomy 8:16)*

Much more can be learned from this remarkable man's life; I've only begun to scratch the surface. In our next chapter we'll look into one other vital act in Abraham's life.

NINETEEN

The First Mention of Worship

The first mention of *worship* in the Bible is in reference to Abraham. God seeks those who will worship Him—it's the ultimate ministry we can bring to God. But what exactly is worship? I vividly recall my father sharing how, during the course of his seventy years of ministry, he'd been privileged to speak at a number of Bible College campuses, as well as Seminaries. He would often look through their syllabus to see what courses were offered. He then remarked that he had seen plenty of courses on music, but never a course on worship.

You can learn to play an instrument, or take singing lessons, yet never learn the art of worship— because worship transcends music. Not everyone is called to be an apostle, prophet, evangelist, pastor or teacher, but everyone is called to be a worshipper. Therefore, let's look at eight facets of worship:

- The PRIORITY of Worship
- The PERSON of Worship
- The PROVISION of Worship
- The PICTURE of Worship
- The PRICE of Worship
- The POSTURE of Worship
- The PURITY of Worship
- The POWER of Worship

The PRIORITY of Worship

A.W. Tozer said this concerning worship: "God wants worshippers before workers; indeed the only acceptable workers are those who have learned the art of worship." Tozer also wrote: "We are called to an everlasting preoccupation with God . . . Man was made to worship God. God gave to man a harp and said, 'Here, above all the creatures that I have made, I have given you the largest "HARP." You can worship Me in a manner that no other creature can.' And when he sinned, man took that instrument and threw it down in the mud."

Don't be confused by Tozer's use of the word HARP, as though worship was confined solely to the realm of music. The greatest acts of worship recorded in the Bible are not associated with music.

That doesn't mean we cannot use music in our worship—we most certainly can.

T. Austin Sparks wrote: "The beginning of everything in relation to God is worship; that is, God having the central and supreme place of recognition, of acknowledgment, of government . . . God having the supreme right in our complete obedience and surrender—in every part and phase of our being. Worship begins there. It's a relationship, not only an exercise. It's not something that we do in specified ways and methods; it's an attitude of life, a place which God has in the entire consciousness . . . that is worship."

Jesus summed it all up when He said, *"I do only do the things that please the Father."* That is true worship!

The PERSON of Worship

Worship must have a focus. Jesus told the woman of Samaria at the well, *"You worship that which you do not know, we worship that which we know . . ."* (John 4:22) Prior to this, the woman explained that her people worshipped on "this mountain." Jesus explained that worship had nothing to do with a place, but was about a person. *" . . . an hour is coming, and now is, when the true worshippers shall worship the Father . . ."* (John 4:23) We need to guard against the *means and methods* of worship; we cannot allow them to eclipse the OBJECT of worship. It's not the chord structure, or the range of one's voice, but the condition of the heart that determines our worship. The Psalmist penned these words: *"Ascribe to the Lord the glory due His name. Worship the Lord in the beauty of holiness." (Psalm 29:2)* In another Psalm he wrote: *"Exalt the Lord our God and worship at His footstool." (Psalm 99:5)* We read throughout the Psalms that our worship is always directed toward a person, God Himself.

The PROVISION of Worship

Charles Spurgeon said of worship: "It is the work of the Spirit in the soul, returning to its author." In the Book of Ecclesiastes we read: *"All the streams flow into the sea, yet the sea is never full. To the place from which they flow, the streams flow back again." (Ecclesiastes 1:7)* The writer understood this constant cycle of evaporation and precipitation. Waters evaporate and become clouds, which release the rains and create rivers that flow into the sea, there to be evaporated again. Our worship, likewise, consists of giving back to God a heart of deep appreciation for all His blessing that He bestows on us morning by morning. Paul explained it this way: *"For from Him and through Him and to Him are all things. To Him be the glory forever. Amen." (Romans 11:36)* Paul asked the Corinthians, *"What do you have that you did nor receive?" (1 Corinthians 4:7)* Worship consists of acknowledging God as the source of all our blessings and benefits.

The PICTURE of Worship

There's no better picture of worship than that of Abraham and Isaac. We've already seen Abraham's willingness to respond in obedience to God's call to leave behind his country, relatives and his father's house. Abraham passed these tests with flying colors, proving that his love for God surpassed his love of these other things. But years went by, and Abraham didn't see the fulfillment of God's promise of a son. His wife Sarah was now well past the age of childbearing. So Abraham took matters into his own hands, fathering a child through his servant Hagar. However, God is faithful to His promise—Sarah conceived and together they had a son, Isaac.

Abraham and Isaac became inseparable; Isaac was the love of his father's life. As the bond between father and son grew, God decided to see if Abraham's love for Isaac exceeded his love for Him. God told Abraham, *"Take now you son, your only son, whom you love, Isaac, and go to the land of Moriah; and offer him there as a burnt offering on one of the mountains of which I will tell you."* (Genesis 22:2) Immediately following God's command we read: *"So Abraham arose early in the morning . . . and went to the place of which the Lord had told him."* (Genesis 22:3) What a response! *He rose early . . .* This phrase tells volumes about Abraham. According to God, this character trait was one of the reasons He chose Abraham in the first place. *"For I have chosen him, in order that he may command his children and his household after him to keep the way of the Lord by doing righteousness and justice; in order that the Lord may bring upon Abraham what He has spoken about him."* *(Genesis 18:19)*

Abraham's radical obedience was one of his greatest qualities. Without any delay or hesitation, Abraham responded to God's call to offer up his only son. After three days of travel, Abraham came to the designated mountain and told his servants, *"Stay here with the donkey, and I and the lad will go yonder, and we will worship and return to you." (Genesis 22:5)* This is the first time we read the word *worship* in the Bible. Notice that there's no choir singing in the background to create a *spiritual atmosphere*. There's no mention of music or instruments—just two radically obedient children, faithfully fulfilling their Father's orders. Abraham said, *"I and the lad will go yonder, and WE will worship."* Both father and son *worshipped*. Noah Webster, in his 1828 Dictionary, defines *worship* this way: *To honor with extravagant love and extreme submission.* The picture of Abraham offering up Isaac is where Webster derived his definition of worship.

Worship involves extravagance—nothing is withheld, but all is lavishly and abundantly poured out. Extreme submission involves unquestionable obedience, regardless of personal pain or loss. I love the way the Isaac Watt's hymn expressed it:

"Were the whole realm of nature mine,
That were a present far too small;
Love so amazing, so divine,
Demands my soul, my life, my all."

God's word commands us to love the Lord our God with *all of our heart*. Remember, the first three mentions of the word *heart* in the Scriptures spoke of our minds, wills and emotions. God is after our heart. Abraham had to surrender his *mind* to God's plan. It didn't make any sense to kill his son. After all, this was the child of promise, without whom God's promises couldn't be fulfilled. Abraham also surrendered his *will*. No caring father, in the natural, could be convinced to willingly offer up his child. Instead he would do everything to protect the one he loved. Finally, Abraham had to surrender his *emotions*.. It's relatively easy to surrender something you have little or no attachment to. But God knew how much he loved Isaac. And yet, Abraham's heart was fixed on pleasing God, and not self.

As we know, God provided a ram as a substitute for Isaac; it was caught in the thicket by the horns — this would have been the only way the ram would be acceptable as an offering. The horns wouldn't be damaged, whereas anywhere else on the animal the thorns of the thicket would have wounded or scarred it, thereby rendering it unfit for a sacrifice. What a perfect *type* of the Lord Jesus Christ, who knew no sin yet became sin for us, that we might be the righteousness of God.

The PRICE of Worship

As we've seen, true worship is costly. I'm reminded of the woman who came to Jesus with an alabaster box of expensive perfume; it was worth 300 denarii — the equivalent of a year's salary. If you remove fifty-two Sabbaths, plus the feast days, you are left with around three hundred days of work per year. What a beautiful illustration of worship as she poured it out on the Lord, filling the house with its fragrance. Consider also the widow woman who gave all she had into the treasury. In comparison to the woman with the alabaster, she gave virtually nothing. Yet Jesus wasn't looking at the amount, but at her heart.

A true worshipper doesn't consider the price, but the value of the person. A man will save thousands of dollars to buy his dream car, boat, or motorcycle, only to fall madly in love with the woman of his dreams. He then thinks nothing of spending all he has on an engagement ring, never shedding a tear. Why? Because the object of his love matters more to him than the price he must pay. When Ornan the Jebusite offered to give David his threshing floor as a gift, to build an altar upon (to stop the plague David caused), David insisted on buying the land instead, saying, *"No, but I will surely buy it from you for a price, for I will not offer burnt offerings to the Lord my God which cost me nothing."* (2 Samuel 24:24) But I believe David's greatest act of worship was immediately following the death of his infant son (born to Bathsheba). Because of David's sin of adultery, murder and reproach on God's name, God took the life of the child. After days of fasting and prayer, hoping God would spare the child, David rose from prayer after learning the child was dead. *"So David arose from the ground, washed, anointed himself, and changed his clothes; and he came into the house of the Lord and worshipped."* (2 Samuel 12:20) This was costly worship indeed. David was emotionally torn apart by the loss of his child, and yet he chose to worship God regardless of his feelings. Our circumstances may change, but God's *WORTHship* is unchangeable.

Worship can be summed up in the word *amen*. Kittle, in his *Theological Dictionary of The New Testament*, defines the word "amen" to means: "Concurring with, or to be in full agreement or committed to." A worshipper, then, is in full agreement with the will of God, regardless of personal loss or pain. His heart responds, *Amen, amen, amen!*

The POSTURE of Worship

Worship is always expressed by falling down, bowing, kneeling or prostrating ourselves. The Psalmist wrote: *"Come let us worship and bow down; let us kneel before the Lord our God our Maker."* (Psalm 95:6) We see this also when the Magi arrived at the place where Jesus lay: *"The Magi fell down and worshipped the Christ child." (Matthew 2:11)* The posture of bowing, kneeling or prostrating yourself is a sign that you're placing yourself in a lower position and showing respect for the one you acknowledge as far superior in person, position and power. As John the Baptist said: *"He must increase, but I must decrease." (John 3:30)*

The PURITY of Worship

Jesus said that those who worship the Father *"must worship Him in spirit and in truth." (John 4:24)* The Samaritan woman he was speaking to had tried differentiating between their mountain and Jerusalem. But as I mentioned before, Jesus (in essence) told her that it's not about a *place,* but a *person.* Here is how G. Campbell Morgan expounds these verses: "Thus He answered her, in statements so profound that sometimes I think we hardly yet grasp their significance. He revealed the fact that there's no value in Jerusalem, apart from the reality and spiritual intention. The hour cometh and now is, when they that worship God, worship in spirit and truth. It's not a question of locality in worship. Moreover it's not a question of intellect merely. To worship, men must get down to the deepest thing in their personality, spirit and truth. There must be honesty; there must be reality. As though He had said to her, I've been trying to help you there, by tearing off the mask, and compelling you to face your own life. If you are prepared to do that, you need not discuss locations. Gerizim is nothing; Jerusalem is nothing; spirit and truth are everything." *(The Four Gospels, G. Campbell Morgan. Oliphants LTD, London. The Gospel According To John, page 76.)*

The incense offered in the Tabernacle of old ascended to God from the Altar of Incense. The coals were taken from the Brazen Altar. Any other incense was considered *strange fire*. Likewise, the only acceptable worship must be based upon the Cross. The writer to Hebrews states it like this: *"Through Him then, let us continually offer up a sacrifice of praise to God, that is the fruit of lips that give thanks to His name."* (Hebrews 13:15) There can be no acceptable sacrifice or worship unless it's THROUGH HIM. Our worship is derived from who God is and what He has done. Therefore, clean hands and a pure heart are essential if our worship is going to be acceptable. As the Psalmist so aptly put it: *"Thou dost desire truth in the innermost being."* *(Psalm 51:6)*

The POWER of Worship

The true worshipper is *dead to self* and *alive to God*. Their life revolves around honoring and glorifying God in everything they say and do. They no longer regard reputation, position, or attainment as important as they do *pleasing God*.

Once a person has become a true worshipper, God is able to entrust them with everything.

Consider these words: *"For the eyes of the Lord move to and fro throughout the earth that He may strongly support those whose heart is continually His."* (2 Chronicles 16:9) God makes it absolutely clear that His power — or "strong support" — is given to those whose *heart* is completely His. Worship is a HEART condition and has little to do with talent or craft. We are to *"worship the Lord in Holy attire."* (Psalm 96:9) Holy attire is *'to put on the Lord Jesus Christ and make no provision for the flesh.(Romans 13:14)*

TWENTY

The First House of God

Abraham, Isaac and Jacob are referred to as "the fathers." These three men were foundational to the formation of Israel as a nation. Jacob, to say the least, was an interesting character. While I have no intention of exploring his life in great detail, I do want to focus on one particular (brief but important) episode in his life: After leaving his home, on the advice of his father, Jacob traveled to his uncle Laban's house in search of a wife. Before reaching his destination, he spent a night alone in the open, near the city of Luz. Scripture says: *"And he came to a certain place and spent the night there, because the sun had set; and he took one of the stones of the place and put it under his head, and lay down in that place." (Genesis 28:11)* (Before going any further, jump to the end of the story and notice that God visited Jacob in a dream and he named the place Bethel, meaning *the house of God*. Now return to the beginning.) In verse eleven we're told three times that Jacob *came to a place*. There's nothing significant about this place. It isn't described as special or famous. All we're told is that it was *a certain place*.

What changed this ordinary spot into *the house of God?* There was no tabernacle or temple there. In fact there was no structure whatsoever. There was nothing there except a few loose stones, and Jacob used one as a pillow. So what transformed this place from being totally insignificant to being awesome? The presence of God. *"Surely the Lord is in this place." (Verse 16)* Because this is the very first mention of the *House of God* after the fall, it gives us some understanding of what we should expect the *House of God* to be in our day.

LESSON #1:
Without the *presence of God* there is no House of God — all you have is a place.

That place may be a magnificent cathedral towering above the surrounding buildings. People may come from around the world to view its magnificent architecture and stained glass windows, but without the presence of God it's just a place.

LESSON #2:
The House of God should *connect earth with heaven.*

In his dream Jacob sees a ladder reach from earth to heaven. A ladder, in the natural, gives you access to places you can't reach alone. I have a ladder in my garage that I use when I can't reach where I need to be. Jacob saw only one ladder, not several. There is access only through our Lord and Savior Jesus Christ. He declared, *"I am the way . . . no one comes to the Father, but through Me."* (John 14:6) Recently I picked up an old daily devotional book and read these words: "A way always leads somewhere; Jesus is the way from earth to heaven, and also from heaven to earth. Through Him we get to God, and through Him God comes to us. He is the true and only ladder whose foot rests on the earth, and whose top reaches up to the very glory of God. In His humanity Jesus comes down to the lowest depths of human need and sorrow. Had He been God only, and not man, He couldn't have done that. The incarnation was the letting of the ladder down until it rested in the deepest valleys. There's no spot of shame or guilt in this world from which there is not a ladder of light, with its celestial steps leading upward to God in heaven . . . A ladder is a way to climb: Christ is the way, and therefore by which sinners can go up out of their sins to the purity and blessedness of heaven."

135

LESSON #3:
The House of God was a place of
supernatural activity.

There were angels ascending and descending. These supernatural beings are sent forth on behalf of all heirs of salvation. Do we really believe God is present when we gather together? If not, we don't have a church—we just have a place. If God's presence is in His House, then we should expect supernatural activity to take place.

God is here!
We have His guarantee
Where two or three are gathered,
That's where He said He'd be.
Yes, God is here.
The One who made the universe is here,
The one who walked on water,
And made the blind to see,
Is standing here among us
In all His majesty.
God is here!

LESSON #4:
The House of God was a place of *revelation.*

God spoke to Jacob and revealed who He was. *"I am the Lord, the God of your father Abraham and the God of Isaac . . ."* When God reveals Himself, He is always consistent with His past. Anytime a new "revelation" of God doesn't conform to His past "ways," we must immediately reject such a revelation as false. God never changes or updates His profile. He doesn't keep abreast with our culture. Paul reminds Timothy of this when he admonishes him with these words: *"In case I am delayed, I write so that you may know how one ought to conduct himself in the household of God, which is the church of the living God, the pillar and support of the truth."* (1 Timothy 3:15) God's truth never changes; every revelation must be tested with God's Word.

LESSON #5:
God's House should be a place where we
hear from God.

Regarding the place Jacob called the House of God, we read in Genesis Twenty-Eight: " . . . *the Lord stood above it and said* . . ." Imagine going to someone's house and seeing the one whose house you entered sitting there silently the whole time. You would probably feel very strange and uncomfortable. But do we go to God's house expecting Him to speak to us? God's House was referred to later as the "Tent of Meeting."

LESSON #6:
The House of God became *a place of vision.*

God revealed to Jacob His plan to reach the nations of the earth through him and his seed. Shouldn't we go to the House of God to hear from heaven as to His assignment for our lives?

LESSON #7:
Jacob tells us that God's House *"is the gate of heaven."*

Gates speak of authority. Jesus declared, *"I will build My church, and the gates of hell shall not over-power it." (Matthew 16:18)* Do we really believe that God's church has all the authority in heaven and earth backing it? We should gather as a church with the belief that as a body rightly related to our head, the Lord Jesus Christ, we have all authority.

LESSON #8:
The House of God should be a place of *vows or commitment.*

It's impossible to have a genuine meeting with God and remain as we were. When Paul met Christ on that Damascus road he immediately cried, *"Lord, what do you want me to do?"* Jacob, likewise, vowed to God that from henceforth: *"The Lord will be my God." (Verse 21)*

LESSON #9:
God's House became a place of *separation.*

When Jacob returned to Bethel, at the command of the Lord, he told his household, *"Put away the foreign gods which are among you, and purify yourselves and change your garments . . ."* (Genesis 35:2) Jacob was well aware of the fact that God's House was to be free from mixture of any type. All other gods had to be put away and purity was God's absolute standard.

LESSON #10:
God's House requires *an altar.*

We never read of God's House without it having an altar. The altar was the place of sacrifice and surrender, where the very best was given to God.

LESSON #11:
God's House was a place of *transformation.*

We read: *"God appeared to Jacob again . . . and God said to him . . . you shall no longer be called Jacob, but Israel shall be your name . . ."* (Genesis 35:10) It's impossible to have a meeting place with God and not be changed. God's house should be a place where old things pass away and all things become new!

Take time to ponder and meditate on Bethel, the House of God. We too easily accept complacency as the norm; what an insult to the Living God in whom we live and move and have our very being.

All of these lessons we've looked at can be found later in God's Tabernacle and Temple. I've tried to challenge your thinking regarding the House of God; I need to remind you that God's House is no longer found in a *place*, but in a *person* – or a group of persons. *"The God who made the world and all things in it, since He is Lord of heaven and earth, does not dwell in temples made with hands; neither is He served by human hands, as though He needed anything, since He Himself gives to all life and breath and all things."* *(Acts 17:24-25)* When we transition from the Old Testament to the New, we no longer read of God's dwelling being a physical place, but rather a spiritual place. *"Or do you not know that your body is a temple of the Holy Spirit who is in you, whom you have from God . . ."* *(1 Corinthians 6:19)* *"If anyone loves Me, he will keep My word; and My Father will love him, and We will come and make Our abode in him."* *(John 14:23)* With this in mind, I believe that what Jacob experienced at Bethel can also be applied to our lives.

TWENTY-ONE

The First Commission

In light of the *Gentile Roots of the Jewish Faith*, what do you suppose God's divine purpose was for creating the nation of Israel? Scripture reveals that long before Israel ever existed, God revealed to Abraham, Isaac and Jacob His intentions regarding this new nation. When God first appeared to Abraham, He promised that not only was He going to bless him, but also through him all the families of the earth would be blessed. God repeated this three times to Abraham and also gave Isaac and Jacob the same promise. In this promise God revealed His heart for *all* nations. There's no question that while God's heart was broken over man's selfishness and sin, God also sought to reveal to men His love, mercy, forgiveness and compassion. With this in mind, He determined to raise up a nation that would partner with Him to reach the nations.

When God told Abraham, Isaac and Jacob that through their seed all nations would be blessed, what did He mean by the term *blessed?* To understand this word, we turn to Paul's letter to the Galatians; Paul gives us an illustration of what God meant: *"And the Scripture, foreseeing that God would justify the Gentiles by faith, preached the gospel beforehand to Abraham, saying, 'All THE NATIONS SHALL BE BLESSED IN YOU.'"* We see then that the word "blessed" pertained to their salvation. Allow me to back that up with another verse. In Acts we read these words (addressed to Israel): *"It is you who are the sons of the prophets, and of the covenant that God made with your fathers, saying to Abraham, 'AND IN YOUR SEED ALL THE FAMILIES OF THE EARTH SHALL BE BLESSED.' For you first God raised up His Servant (Jesus), and sent Him to* **bless** *you by turning every one of you from your wicked ways."* (Acts 3:25-26) *[Emphasis mine.]* Once more, the word *bless* or *blessed* referred to God's desire to see the nations saved, forgiven, redeemed or justified. These promises were given long before Israel existed as a nation. It was God's intention to create a "servant nation" that would carry out His purpose.

Later God declared through His prophet Isaiah: *"You are My servant Israel, In whom I will show My glory . . . I will also make you a light to the nations, so*

that My salvation may reach to the ends of the earth."
(Isaiah 49:3,8)

Without laboring this point, let me just say that throughout Israel's history, God had men who understood His intention for their nation. Yes, God promised to bless them, but also (through them) to bless the world. David understood this when he wrote Psalm Sixty-Seven: *"God be gracious to us and bless us, And cause His face to shine upon us – that Thy way may be known on the earth, Thy salvation among all nations . . . God. Our God, blesses us, God blesses us, that all the ends of the earth may fear Him."* Not only did David ask for God's blessing upon Israel, but also that God's blessing would be a testimony to ALL nations, resulting in their salvation. David had a clear understanding of God's purpose for Israel.

David's son Solomon also understood what God's mind was pertaining to God's house or Temple. At the dedication of Solomon's Temple, Solomon has fulfilled his father David's desire to build God a habitation worthy of Him. Solomon spreads out his hands in prayer and, after praying for his own people, says: *"Also concerning the foreigner who is not of Thy people Israel, when he comes from a far country for Thy great name's sake and Thy mighty hand and Thine outstretched arm, when they come and pray toward this house, then hear Thou from heaven, from Thy dwelling place, and do according to all for which the foreigner calls to Thee, in order that all the peoples of the earth may know Thy name."* *(2 Chronicles 6:32-33)* This

is one of the most revelatory passages in the Old
Testament. Solomon understood that God's house
wasn't just for his own people, but it was to be a
house of prayer for all nations. He anticipated God's
glory filling His house so that the nations would
hear of God's presence and power residing there. In
turn Solomon saw them coming because they had
heard of God's greatness and were seeking Him to
meet their needs. Solomon said to God, *When you
answer the foreigner's prayers then ALL the ends of the
earth will hear about it.* Throughout Israel's history
there were men who aligned themselves with the
divine purpose. However, Israel failed to grasp
their purpose. They chose to live selfishly, oblivious
to the needs of the nations around them. Not only
did they fail to fulfill their God-given purpose and
destiny, but also they chose to defile themselves
with the gods of the very people they were raised
up to reach.

In the book of Romans we read these words: *"For
I say that Christ has become a servant to the circumci-
sion on behalf of the truth of God to confirm the promises given to the fathers." (Romans 15:8)* We learn here
that one of the reasons Jesus came was to *confirm
the promises* given to the fathers. When we read the
word *fathers*, it always refers to Abraham, Isaac and
Jacob. And so we're told that Jesus came to confirm
or establish the promises God made to these three
men. The following verses show that these promises were regarding the nations—Gentiles or

unsaved—these all being one and the same. Let's continue reading: " . . . *and for the Gentiles to glorify God for His mercy, as it's written, 'Therefore, I will give praise to thee among the Gentiles, and I will sing to thy name.' And again He says, 'REJOICE O GENTILES, WITH HIS PEOPLE.' And again, 'PRAISE THE LORD ALL YOU GENTILES, AND LET ALL THE PEOPLE PRAISE HIM.'"*

Though Israel had long forgotten their calling, God had not forgotten. He came to re-establish His promises. Let's examine exactly what God meant when He told Abraham, Isaac and Jacob *"through your **seed"*** all the nations of the earth would be blessed. *(See Genesis 12:3, 18:18, 22:18, 26:4, 28:14)* Unfortunately, some translations use the word *descendants* instead of *seed*. What was God referring to when He used the word *seed*? To find out we turn again to the book of Galatians: *"Now the promises were spoken to Abraham and to his seed. He does not say, 'And to seeds,' as referring to many, but rather to one, 'And to your seed,' that is, Christ." (Galatians 3:16)* Perhaps you're sighing in relief, thinking *That lets me off the hook!* Hold on a minute; we're not finished reading yet. Paul continues, *"For you are all sons of God through faith in Christ Jesus. For all of you who were baptized into Christ have clothed yourself with Christ. There is neither Jew nor Greek, there is neither slave nor free man, there is neither male nor female; for you are all one in Christ Jesus. And if you belong to Christ,* *then you are Abraham's offspring, heirs according to promise." (Galatians 26:29)*

An heir is one who inhcrits something. According to these verses we inherit the promises given to Abraham. Some groups within the Body of Christ claim just one portion of the promise, namely, *"I will bless you."* They fail to claim the rest of the promise: *" . . . that through you all the families of the earth shall be blessed."* They selfishly choose the *benefits* of the promises, but ignore the responsibility of reaching out to the families (or nations) of the earth, which were also part of the promise.

By now you may be asking, *What about Israel?* I'm glad you asked. Matthew records that Jesus went into the Temple one day; the chief priest and elders of the people were gathered there — all of the spiritual leaders of Israel were present. Jesus then shared a parable with them about a certain landowner who planted a vineyard, fully expecting to receive a harvest in due season. The landowner took great care for his vineyard by protecting it with a wall, as well as watching over it from a tower. He dug a winepress in order to partake of the fruit of the vine. The owner patiently waited until harvest time and then sent his slaves to gather in the harvest. Those responsible for the vineyard beat one slave, killed another and stoned the third. When the owner found out what happened to his slaves, he sent even more slaves. But they were mistreated in the same way. Finally the owner decided to send his son, expecting them to treat his son with the respect he deserved. Tragically, they killed the son also and seized the vineyard for themselves.

The parable needs no interpretation. The vineyard represents Israel. God took great care of His people by protecting and watching over them. His plan was to reap a harvest of souls through them. The slaves He sent represent the numerous prophets whom were sent to denounce sin and keep Israel on track with God's purpose. But Israel, not wanting to obey or be involved in God's purpose, stoned anyone who stood in way of their plans. God's incredible patience is revealed when He sent a larger group of prophets—immediately after they had stoned the first group. The son in the parable obviously speaks of Christ, who they rejected and crucified.

When the leaders of the nation heard this parable, Jesus asked them what they would do if the owner of the vineyard came. They responded that, if they owned the vineyard, they would destroy those workers and replace them with workers who would give the owner His due—a harvest. As they failed to understand that Jesus was referring to *them* as the vineyard, He declared: *"Therefore I say to you, the Kingdom of God will be taken away from you, and given to a nation producing the fruit of it."* (*Matthew 21:43*)

But what *nation* was the Lord referring to? In First Peter we read: *"But you are A CHOSEN RACE,*

A ROYAL PRIESTHOOD, A HOLY NATION, A PEOPLE FOR GOD'S OWN POSSESSION, that you may proclaim the excellencies of Him who has called you out of darkness into His marvelous light; for you once were NOT A PEOPLE, but now you are THE PEOPLE OF GOD; you had NOT RECEIVED MERCY, but now you HAVE RECEIVED MERCY." (1 Peter 2:9-10) *[Emphasis mine.]* These verses clearly pertain to *every believer*. But before rejoicing in the grace of God, keep in mind that we too are Abraham's seed — we inherit not only the blessing of God (salvation), but also the responsibility that goes with it.

Before writing what we've just read, Peter stated: *"And coming to Him as to a living stone, rejected by men but choice and precious in the sight of God, you also as living stones, are being built up as a spiritual house for a holy priesthood, to offer up spiritual sacrifices, acceptable to God through Jesus Christ."* (1 Peter 2:4-5) Thankfully, under the New Covenant we no longer approach God by bringing Him some type of animal sacrifice. Jesus Christ met all of those conditions for us. However, we do need to bring "spiritual sacrifices." Most believers understand this and are acquainted with most of these sacrifices. The first one that comes to mind is the *sacrifice of praise*. Then there's the sacrifice of our whole body to God, as a *living sacrifice*. There's also the sacrifice of monetary gifts, our *tithes and offerings*. But then there's the rarest sacrifice, one we often fall short of: *the sacrifice of souls*. Paul the apostle understood this sacrifice; listen to these words from his testimony: *"But I have written very boldly to you on some points, so as to remind you again, because of the grace that was given me from God, to be a minister of Jesus Christ to the Gentiles, ministering as a priest the gospel of God, that my offering of the Gentiles might become acceptable, sanctified by the Holy Spirit." (Romans 15:15-16)* Paul explains here that (as a priest) one of the offerings he brought to God was *a repentant sinner.*

I believe this offering thrills the heart of God more than any other offering or sacrifice. Jesus said, *"There is more joy in heaven over one sinner who repents . . ." (Luke 15:7)* Keep in mind that as A HOLY NATION we're to *proclaim* the excellencies of Him who called us out of darkness . . ." This is often referred to as THE ABRAHAMIC COVENANT, God's longing to reach mankind with the gospel or *blessing.*

Before we close, I want to look at what I believe to be one of the most important passages in the entire Bible. At the end of Luke's gospel, Chapter Twenty-Four, Jesus has risen from the grave and is meeting with His disciples. He asks for something to eat and then tells them that everything written in the Law of Moses and the Prophets and the Psalms *must be fulfilled.* The Law of Moses refers to the first five books of the Bible, the Prophets the bulk of the Bible, and the Psalms are the poetic books. In essence, Jesus was saying that everything in the Bible must be fulfilled. (Remember there was no

New Testament at this time.) We're told that Jesus then *"opened their minds to understand the Scriptures."* Imagine sitting at the feet of the *Living Word*, the Word that became flesh — the greatest teacher of all time — and hearing Him open up the Scriptures to you. Here is where it gets very interesting: Jesus is about to summarize the entire Scriptures in just two verses. Wow! *"And He said to them, 'Thus it is written, that the Christ (the Seed) should suffer and rise again from the dead the third day; and that repentance for forgiveness of sins should be proclaimed in His name to all nations, beginning from Jerusalem.'" (Verses 46-47)*

Do you see how these verses capsulize the heart of God for the lost, for all nations? Jesus then told His disciples, *"You are witnesses of these things, and behold I am sending forth the promise of My Father upon you; but you are to stay in the city until you are clothed with power from on high." (Verse 48-49)* Israel, as a whole, failed to respond to God's purpose. Yet here Jesus is meeting with eleven Jewish disciples, charging them with the same commission He gave to the twelve tribes.

We must always remember that we're incapable of doing God's will in our own strength. That is why Jesus told His disciples to wait for the promised Holy Spirit who would empower them for the task. In case I've not made myself clear, we, as believers, are also called to reach every creature with the gospel. As God's HOLY NATION, this is also our commission. We are to proclaim the goodness of Him who called us out of darkness into His marvelous light.

Please read the Appendix at the close of this book regarding Israel's current role.

TWENTY-TWO

The First Passover

Our brief journey through Genesis is almost over. In this chapter I want to take you to the book of Exodus as we look at Israel's very first feast—the Feast of Passover. We're now leaving the Book of Genesis and its beginnings of Gentile roots. In many ways, the Passover was the beginning of Israel's existence as a nation. Although Israel existed for four hundred years in Egypt, only after their deliverance from the house of bondage did they become a recognized nation, having their own laws and government. In a spiritual sense, this is also true about each of us. We existed prior to our acceptance of Christ as Lord and Savior, but it wasn't until we applied the blood of the Lamb to our lives that we really began life as God intended.

Likewise, Israel's transformation began with the Feast of Passover. This feast was the first of seven feasts that Israel celebrated yearly. The parallels between this feast and the believer's deliverance from the bondage of sin are clearly evident, as we'll see. I'm going to summarize each aspect of their deliverance under one succinct heading. Paul reminds us, in First Corinthians Chapter Five, verse seven: *"Christ our Passover has been sacrificed."* As you may know, the types and shadows of the Old Testament have their fulfillment in Christ. With that in mind, I want compare the Old with the New — because *"these things were written for our instruction."*

The Bible is made up of numerous books all having one common theme: Christ. Jesus said, *"In the roll of the book it is written of Me." (Hebrews 10:7)* The Apostle Paul, in his letter to the Colossians, wrote: *"Let no one act as a judge in respect to a festival (feast) or a new moon or a Sabbath day which are a mere shadow of things to come but the substance belongs to Christ." (Colossians 2:16-17)* One of my old teachers use to say, "The Old is in the New revealed; the New is in the Old concealed," or "The Old is in the New explained; the New is in the Old contained." Let's study the feast of Passover to examine this wonderful truth.

As we dissect this chapter, the first thing we notice is God saying to Moses and Aaron, *"This month shall be the beginning of months for you. It is to be the first month of the year to you." (Verse 2)*

INAUGURATION: *A ceremony to mark the beginning of something new.* This feast was to commence the beginning of a NEW YEAR, or a new season of their life. They were about to slay the lamb as the means of their deliverance (more on that later). The New Testament fulfillment of this feast was, *"For Christ our Passover also has been sacrificed."* *(1 Corinthians 5:7)* Isn't it fascinating that no matter which country you travel to—whether it be Socialistic, Communistic, Atheistic, Muslim or Hindu—they all use the same measurement of time? Today is the year 2018 A.D. In Latin the A.D. stands for Anno Domini—*The Year of Our Lord.* Yes, Jesus our Passover Lamb divided time, and the whole world acknowledges it without even being aware of it. Every believer who places their trust in Christ also begins a new season or new year in their life. Old things pass away and all things become new. We begin a new life as we are born anew by the Spirit of God.

God then tells Moses to speak to the congregation of Israel saying, *"On the tenth of this month they are each one to take a lamb for themselves, according to their father's household, a lamb for each household."* *(Verse 3)*

SUBSTITUTION: *A person used in place of another.* The lamb was their substitute, taking their place in death. *"Behold the Lamb of God that takes away the sin* *of the world." (John 1:29)* The hymn writer penned it this way:

> *In my place condemned He stood,*
> *Sealed my pardon with His blood.*
> *Hallelujah what a Savior.*

INSPECTION: *"Your lamb shall be an unblemished male a year old . . ." (Verse 5)* Every lamb had to be examined or inspected before it could be sacrificed. If any blemish was found it was rejected. Before Jesus was crucified He was examined both by Pilate and Herod and found to be innocent of all charges brought against Him. *"Pilate summoned the chief priests and rulers and the people and said to them, 'You brought this man to me as one who incites the people to rebellion, and behold having examined Him before you, I have found no guilt in this man regarding the charges which you make against Him. No, nor has Herod . . ."* *(Luke 23:13-15)* We read in First Peter: *"You were not redeemed with perishable things like silver and gold... but with the precious blood of a lamb unblemished and spotless." (1 Peter 1:18-19)*

AFFECTION: *A fond or tender feeling toward someone or something.* After each household had selected an unblemished lamb, they were to keep it for four days. *"And you shall keep it until the fourteenth day of the month . . ." (Exodus 12:6)* The lamb was to live among them. John tells us: *"And I saw between the* throne and the elders a Lamb standing as if slain . . ." (Revelation 5:6) The word John uses for *lamb* is the Greek word "arnios" — meaning, a little pet lamb. We're told that Jesus was *"wounded in the house of His friends." (Zechariah 13:6)* He was also betrayed by one of His own disciples. Finally we're told, *"He came to His own and those who were His own did not receive Him." (John 1:11)*

EXECUTION: *"Then the whole assembly of the congregation of Israel is to kill it at twilight." (Exodus 12:6)* Jesus was rejected by His own people when they cried, *"Away with Him, away with Him, crucify Him." (John 19:15)* They also declared: *"We do not want this man to reign over us." (Luke 19:14)* Just as the Passover lamb was to be slain at twilight, so too when Jesus died, *"At the sixth hour darkness fell." (Matthew 27:45)*

APPLICATION/APPROPRIATION: Scripture declares that *without the shedding of blood there is no forgiveness of sin.* But even *with* the shedding of blood, there is no forgiveness for those who don't personally appropriate (take and apply) its effectiveness, value or virtue. Similarly, once the Passover lamb was killed, each household had to apply the blood to their own door. If no blood was applied, even though the lamb had been slain, then there could be no deliverance. Just as the blood was placed on the top and sides of the door, we know there is only one door: Jesus said, *"I am the door, by Me if any man enter in he shall be saved." (John 10:9)* Applying the blood was a sign of a person's faith; they obviously believed the blood had the power to save them. *"Moses by faith he kept the Passover and the sprinkling of the blood, so that he who destroyed the first born should not destroy them." (Hebrews 11:26)*

CONFESSION: The blood wasn't applied to the inside of the door but to the exterior. God could easily have seen the blood on the inside, but here lies a great truth: The blood was a witness to the world that those inside had placed their trust in the blood of the Lamb. We often overlook the importance of our public confession of faith. But Scripture tells us: *"If you confess with your mouth Jesus Christ as Lord and believe in your heart that God raised Him from the dead you shall be saved." (Romans 10:9) "Everyone, therefore, who shall confess Me before men, I will also confess him before My Father who is in heaven." (Matthew 10:32)*

IMPARTATION: *"You shall eat the flesh the same night." (Exodus 12:8)* Not only had the blood to be applied but every Israelite was to partake of the body and blood of the lamb. The lamb was to be roasted with fire and then eaten, providing them with strength for the journey ahead. What a beautiful illustration of the believer who has Christ dwelling in them and providing them the strength to do all things. Jesus said, *"Truly, truly, I say to you unless you eat the flesh of the Son of Man and drink His blood you have no life in yourself." (John 6:53)*

SEPARATION: *"Eat it with your loins girded and sandals on your feet . . . eat it in haste . . ." (Exodus 12:11)* The shed blood of the Passover Lamb did not keep them in bondage, but delivered them from it. This became their way of escape from the *house of bondage.* In like manner, the blood of Christ gives us the power to walk in total freedom — leaving behind our old way of life. God wanted His people out of Egypt and free from the taskmasters who enslaved them; the same is true for us today. *"Come out from among them and be separate and touch not the unclean, and I will welcome you and I will be a Father unto you . . ." (2 Corinthians 6:17)* We also should be able to testify to God's delivering power in our own lives, as Paul reminds us: *"For He delivered us from the dominion of darkness, and transferred us to the kingdom of His beloved Son." (Colossians 1:13)*

PROCLAMATION: *"For I will go through the land of Egypt that night . . . and against all the gods of Egypt I will execute judgment — I AM THE LORD!" (Exodus 12:12)* The Passover was also a demonstration of God's superior power over all other *gods,* which were not merely idols of wood or stone. They were demonic powers, capable of supernatural acts, such as turning the magician's rods into serpents. These powers, however, were no match for the Almighty, who demonstrated that He alone is LORD. In the same way, when Jesus Christ died we read: *"When He had disarmed rulers and authorities He made a public display of them, having triumphed over them through Him."* (Colossians 2:15) Again in Ephesians we read of God's great power: *" . . . what is the surpassing greatness of His power toward us who believe. These are in accordance with the working of the strength of His might which He brought about in Christ, when He raised Him from the dead, and seated Him at His right hand in heavenly places, far above all rule and authority and power and dominion and every name that is named, not only in this age, but also in the one to come."* (Ephesians 1:19-21) When we partake of communion together, *"We proclaim the Lord's death until He comes."* (1 Corinthians 11:26) We desperately need to rediscover the power that we can *proclaim* when partaking of the Lord's supper together.

JUSTIFICATION/LIBERATION: *"When I see the blood, I will pass over you and no plague will befall you to destroy you."* (Exodus 12:13) Every Israelite that placed their faith in the atoning blood of the lamb was spared from death. It had nothing to do with their own merit or achievements. They were justified solely through the blood of the lamb, and thereby spared from the wrath that came on households that failed to apply the blood. We read in the New Testament: *"In the forbearance of God He* passed over the sins previously committed." *(Romans 3:25)* Paul goes on to write: *"Much more then, having been justified by His blood shall we be saved from the wrath of God." (Romans 5:9)* As the Children of Israel began their journey that evening, they heard crying and wailing from the homes of the Egyptians, who were mourning the loss of their first born. This was Israel's night of deliverance and liberation. We too have been liberated from the power of sin and its consequences. *"Since the children share in flesh and blood, He Himself likewise also partook of the same, that through death He might render powerless him who had the power of death, that is the devil; and might deliver those who through fear of death were subject to slavery all their lives . . ." (Hebrews 2:14-15)*

CELEBRATION: *"Now this day will be a memorial to you, and you shall celebrate it as a feast to the Lord; throughout your generations." (Exodus 12:14)* Paul wrote to the Corinthians these words: *"For Christ our Passover also has been sacrificed. Let us therefore celebrate the feast . . ." (1 Corinthians 5:7-8)* When we partake of the communion table, we celebrate the fulfillment of all that Christ, our Passover, has done for us. Thank you Lord!

SANCTIFICATION: It was never God's purpose to emancipate His people from the power and tyranny of sin only to have them return to its bondage. Immediately following Israel's deliverance, God instituted another feast – The Feast of Unleavened Bread. It began the very next day and lasted for seven days. The number *seven* speaks of completion, perfection or wholeness. *Leaven,* on the other hand, typified sin and its nature to permeate everything it touched. God told the Children of Israel, *"Seven days you shall eat unleavened bread, but on the first day you shall remove leaven from your houses; for whoever eats any leaven from the first day until the seventh, that person shall be cut off from Israel." (Exodus 12:15)*

Paul told us that in the Corinthian church there was a man who was sexually involved with his father's wife. Although the church knew about it, they were treating the situation as though it didn't really matter. But Paul warned them that this *leaven,* if not removed, would soon permeate the whole church. He warned them: *"Do you not know that a little leaven leavens the whole lump of dough? Clean out the old leaven. For Christ our Passover also has been sacrificed. Let us therefore celebrate the feast not with old leaven, nor with the leaven of malice and wickedness, but with the unleavened bread of sincerity and truth." (1 Corinthians 5:6-8)* I believe the evangelical church today clearly understands the fact that Christ, our Passover, has been sacrificed for us – and that, consequently, we're saved by faith in the finished work of Jesus Christ our Lamb; however, I also believe we've not emphasized enough the importance of removing any leaven from our lives. Failure to do so, as we've read, results in us being, "cut off." I'm well aware this is contrary to the popular teaching of *eternal security*, but I don't believe we should treat it as insignificant. To do so may result in death!

UNIFICATION: *"And the Lord said to Moses and Aaron, 'This is the ordinance of the Passover . . . it is to be eaten in a single house . . . nor are you to break any bone of it.'" (Exodus 12:43-46)* The breaking of a bone, before being killed, would have rendered the lamb blemished, and therefore not suitable as a perfect sacrifice. The breaking of a bone afterward seems to be less of a problem. We know that when Jesus cried out, *"It is finished!"* and yielded up His spirit to the Father, the Roman soldiers came to break His legs in order to speed up the death process. But Jesus was already dead, so we read: *"The soldiers, therefore, came and broke the legs of the first man and the other man who was crucified with Him; but coming to Jesus, when they saw that He was already dead, they did not break His legs . . . For these things came to pass, that the scripture might be fulfilled, 'NOT A BONE OF HIM SHALL BE BROKEN.'" (John 19:32,36) [Emphasis mine.]* From these verses we learn how Jesus, in His death, fulfilled many Scriptures – including this one. I believe also there's another lesson here as well: God desires for His body to be unbroken, united and free from schism or division. This was the prayer of the Lord Jesus to His Father: *" . . . that* *they may be one even as Thou Father art in Me . . ."* *(John 17:21)*

MATURATION/DIRECTION: *"Then they set out . . . The Lord going before them to lead them."* *(Exodus 13:20-21) "Let My people go that they may serve Me."* *(Exodus 8:1)* God didn't deliver His people so that they could wander aimlessly, *doing their own thing*. God wanted to be their Shepherd and to *lead* them. He had a plan and purpose for their lives. He set them free in order that they might *serve* Him. Paul reminded the believers in Thessalonica: " . . . *how you turned to God from idols to serve a living and true God . . ."* *(1 Thessalonians 1:9)* In each stage of Israel's journey – from Egypt, through the wilderness, to the Promised Land – God intended for His people to grow in their knowledge of Him.

In Egypt they learned that He was THE WAY. The problem in Egypt was SIN. In the wilderness they were to know Him as THE TRUTH. The problem in the wilderness was SELF. This was a time when God revealed His ways, His Law and His precepts etc. In Canaan they were to know Him as THE LIFE. They were *"to reign in life"* over their enemies, which were a type of SATAN.

REDEMPTION: *"Until Thy people pass over, O Lord, Until Thy people pass over whom Thou hast purchased."* *(Exodus 15:16)* The truth that we've been *purchased by God* is sadly lacking in our pulpits today. Most professing-believers want to retain control of their own lives and merely hand over their sins to Christ. But Paul reminds us: *"You are not your own; you have been bought with a price."* (1 Corinthians 6:19) Whatever the blood of Christ *cleanses* it also *claims.* This is confirmed by Paul's letter to Titus when he writes: *"Christ Jesus who gave Himself for us that He might redeem us from every lawless deed AND purify for Himself a people for His own possession, zealous for good deeds."* (Titus 2:14) (My book BLOOD BOUGHT deals with the theme of redemption in more detail.)

IMMERSION: *"Then Moses stretched out his hand over the sea; and the Lord swept the sea back by a strong east wind all night, and turned the sea into dry land, so the waters were divided. And the sons of Israel went through the midst of the sea on the dry, and the waters were like a wall to them on their right hand and on their left . . . Then the Lord said to Moses, 'Stretch out your hand over the sea so that the waters may come back over the Egyptians, over their chariots and their horsemen.'"* (Exodus 14:21-22,26) Here is a beautiful example of water baptism. Israel was raised up to newness of life, while those who previously ruled over them perished, their power forever broken. We too have been *"buried with Him through baptism into death, in order that as Christ was raised from the dead through the glory of the Father, so we too might walk in newness of life . . . for sin shall not be master over you, for you are not under law but under grace."* (Romans 6:4,14)

DESTINATION: Long before Israel ever entered the Promised Land, God had already selected a specific place to establish His house and His people. Moses spoke prophetically when he taught Israel to sing to the Lord this song: *"In Thy loving kindness Thou hast led the people whom Thou hast redeemed; in Thy strength Thou has guided them to Thy holy habitation . . . until thy people pass over whom Thou hast purchased. Thou wilt bring them and plant them in the mountain of Thine inheritance, the place O Lord, which Thou hast made for Thy dwelling, the sanctuary, O Lord, which Thy hands have established."* *(Exodus 15:13,16,17)* We know that this mountain was Mt. Zion, the dwelling that God desired above all others and which corresponds to: *"Mount Zion and to the city of the living God, the heavenly Jerusalem . . ."* *(Hebrews 12:22)* Christ, our Passover, marks the beginning of our spiritual journey. We must not lose heart during the journey, but, like those who have gone before us, *" . . . let us run with endurance the race that is set before us, fixing our eyes on Jesus, the author and perfecter of faith . . ."* *(Hebrews 12:1-2)* Mount Zion, our eternal home and the home of our great and glorious King Jesus, awaits all who finish!

Appendix

No doubt some of you are asking, *Do you believe in replacement theology?* Replacement theology basically refers to the belief that the *Church* has taken over the role of *Israel*, and that God has finished with Israel. My answer is no – I do not believe that! I believe in "Continuation Theology." God hasn't changed; He always desired for all nations to know Him. As a whole, Israel failed to make God known, but Jesus chose twelve *Jews* to continue His plan. *"Follow Me and I will make you fishers of men,"* He told them.

Paul, another Jew, also chose to fulfill His God-given calling to reach the lost. We read: *"And the next Sabbath nearly the whole city assembled to hear the word of God. But when the Jews saw the crowd, they were filled with jealousy and began contradicting the things spoken by Paul and were blaspheming. And Paul and Barnabas spoke out boldly and said, 'It was necessary that the word of God should be spoken to you first; since you repudiated it, and judge yourselves unworthy of eternal life, behold we are turning to the Gentiles. For thus the Lord has commanded us [the Jews] 'I HAVE PLACED YOU AS A LIGHT FOR THE GENTILES, THAT YOU SHOULD BRING SALVATION TO THE END OF THE EARTH.' And when the Gentiles heard this, they began rejoicing and glorifying the word of the Lord; and as many as had been appointed to eternal life believed." (Acts 13:44-48) [Emphasis mine.]* Paul made known to the Jews that (as Jews) they were given the task of reaching the Gentiles – but they rejected their calling. Paul and Barnabas, on the other hand, told their fellow Jews that they would fulfill their calling as Jews without them.

I'm well aware that I'm only scratching the surface of this issue here. Suffice to say, the promises given by God to Israel still pertain to Israel and will be fulfilled in God's perfect time.

www.ingramcontent.com/pod-product-compliance
Lightning Source LLC
Chambersburg PA
CBHW051728040426
42447CB00008B/1019